Marx and Democracy with Chinese Characteristics

by
Markus Haunschmid

updated version by Markus Haunschmid (author and publisher)

Vienna, 02..2016

cover created by Isabelle Gärtner (HBLA Steyr, Austria)

special thanks to Sam Lewis (Great Britain) and Liu Hui / 刘翚 (Austria/China) for amendment, *Thomas Haunschmid (Austria) for the organization with the cover design and Felix Wemheuer (Germany) for scientific councelling*

ISBN-13: 978-1518688164

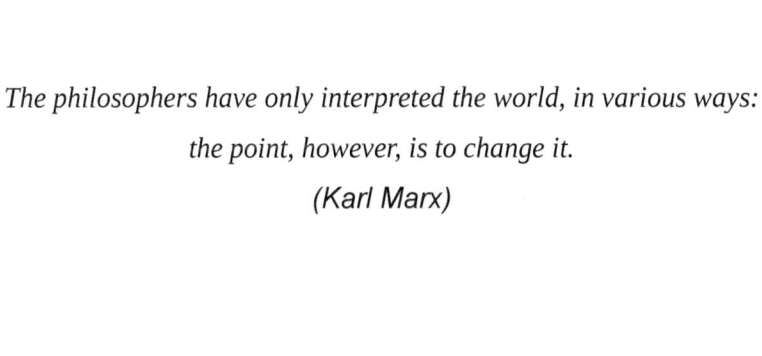

The philosophers have only interpreted the world, in various ways: the point, however, is to change it.

(Karl Marx)

Content

1. Introduction

Orthodox Marxism, therefore, does not imply the uncritical acceptance of the results of Marx's investigations. It is not the 'belief' in this or that thesis, nor the exegesis of a 'sacred' book. On the contrary, orthodoxy refers exclusively to method.

Georg Lukacs[1]

This method is the focus of philosophy regarding the productive class in society; in other words, the subject of Marxist historiography is the proletariat: "that class in society which lives entirely from the sale of its labor and does not draw profit from any kind of capital; whose weal and woe, whose life and death, whose sole existence depends on the demand for labor – hence, on the changing state of business, on the vagaries of unbridled competition. The proletariat, or the class of proletarians, is, in a word, the working class of the 19th

---

[1]

Lukacs, Georg: History and Class Consciousness, Merlin Press, 1967, chapter 1: What is Orthodox Marxism?, p.1   (written in 1919)

century"[2] - and of today. A modern definition of 'working class' includes the traditional industrial worker, as well as migrant workers and people working in services, namely, all those people who have nothing else to sell than their labor force.

In China we face a rapidly growing proletariat - *the* historically revolutionary class, capable of changing the being of man.
Using Marx's method of taking the proletarian class as our foundation is the way to get away from all the metaphysics of science, which take all kinds of other indicators as the basis of their theory except the real lives of men and their productive work, and merely analyzing, rather than interpret.

The majority of intellectuals argued that there were no ideologies any more - with the fall of the Soviet Union, and especially the Berlin Wall in 1989, capitalism became prevalent. "There Is No Alternative" to the capitalist system, short TINA, became the credo of this generation in the Western world. Since the outbreak of the world financial and economic crisis of 2008, the analysis of capitalism by Marx, together

---

[2] Engels, Frederick: The Principles of Communism, 1969 Moscow, Selected Works, Volume One, p. 81-97, Progress Publishers, (original: 1847)

with his proposals of overcoming the predominance of the capitalist system, were en vogue once again. One could say that the conjuncture of Marx's popularity is the reverse of the conjuncture of crisis.

The genuine difference between capitalist democracy and Marxist democracy is the self- responsibility of the individual within the capitalist system, with which comes a division of society, or unity of society, the belief in the "common" in the human being, therefore the scientific method considers "communism" as the basic principle.

Today's principle "divide et impera", divide and rule, broke up society so that nowadays people are reduced to their individual being. While solidarity - the common being and growing of society - does not play any outstanding role in the model of Western democracy as a theoretic construct, Marxist philosophy takes it as given that human beings want to prosper as a species, and offers a scientific method to analyze society on this basis, seeking a pathway - based on this scientific analysis - to achieve an optimal, democratic society based on commonalities.

This thesis focuses on three different terms of democracy:

In Marx' perception of democracy, which he calls true democracy, the element of collectivism - namely society split into micro-groups as a basis for decision making - plays the most important role. It means unity of the universal and the particular, where the state disappears. The modern comprehension of democracy in the Western world was shaped, in reality, by national movements against the monarchy in Europe, including protests for freedom of speech, free press etc.,[3] in a time where most individuals did not have the possibility to participate in the democratic system and were politically suppressed. Since then a reformation of the democratic model has taken place, according to the technological potential of the internet and the material status of the majority of the population, which guarantees enough free time for the majority of the population to participate in political decision-making. While Western democracy focuses on individual rights and freedom, the Chinese perception of democracy concentrated of time on representation of the

---

[3]

Marx and Engels Politische Texte Pressefreiheit und Zensur. Iring Fetscher (editor), Europäische Verlagsanstalt Frankfurt, Europa Verlag Wien, Frankfurt, 1969, p.44-99

collective, especially workers, peasants[4], but also capitalists. The "Three Represents" theory of Jiang Zemin, general secretary of the central committee and president of China in the 1990s, included national capitalists, which he called entrepreneurs, in the theoretic class foundation of the party, arguing that they are an important, productive class. Therefore, we have a combination of Marxist philosophy, watered down with traditional Chinese elements and the political mechanisms of Soviet Russia under Stalin's rule, on a partly national capitalist basis. Under these unique conditions, economically comparable to those of Cuba but on a much bigger scale (1.4 billion people), a new kind of democracy enters the world scene - or can we call it that?

1.1. The connection between language and practice

In my analysis I will focus on the role of democracy and analyze its discourse in the Chinese media, as well as Marx and

---

[4]   It is repeatedly argued that the CCP exercises the democratic dictatorship of the people: "China is a (...) people's democratic dictatorship which is led by the working class and based on the alliance of workers and peasants." (see foot note number 79 on page 47)

Engel's comprehension of it. The role of language in society can be described as quite controversial, especially its practical influence.

In the view of analytic philosophy the fruits of human cognition are expressed by language: studying the world from the angle of language is to grasp it based on the relationship between people. But analytic philosophy, for example discourse analysis, creates an independent realm out of language, focusing on grammar and structure rather than necessity in order to reach a common goal for society. However, Marx states that, "language, like consciousness, only arises from the need, the necessity, of intercourse with other men"; it is the internalization of practice, structured in man's brain, the manifestation of real life, i.e. experiences etc. in our head.[5] Our ideas of the world are shaped by our daily lives and expresses itself in language. So language does not determine practice, but practice does determine language. Only on the

---

[5]   Marx, Karl: A Critique of The German Ideology, written: 1845- 1846, first published in full: 1932, online source: Marx/Engels Internet Archive (marxists.org), published in 2000, http://www.marxists.org/archive/marx/works/1845-gi/part_a.htm (8 of 12), seen 10.2014

fundament of practice can one explain the relationship between man and world.[6]

Hence, language and practice can detach; language does not necessarily have to be connected to real life, human beings have the ability to make up stories and talk about their fantasies and existing things. So this essay seeks to bring the topic of workers democracy back to the material development, taking into account the role of language and the motivation for its use. Rather than taking into account grammar and text structure, the focus lies on the choices of words and their cohesion, in order to find the motive behind the discourse, a tool for legitimacy of power according to the model 'power → discourse → power'.

1.2. The degenerated character of the CCP

The CCP (Communist Party of China) refers to the development of the party's ideas from Marx to Lenin, Stalin, Mao, Deng Xiaoping, Jiang Zemin to Hu Jintao. With every change of government, the ideological direction of the government changes, even though the measures or policies to

---

[6] Yang Geng: Defense for Marx. A New Interpretation of Marxist Philosophy, 2003, Canut Publishers, p.244- 248

pursue the same, theoretical goal are different. Accordingly, the Chinese leadership writes and rewrites its history as the decades pass by. In a profound analysis of the democratic potential of the People's Republic of China, one cannot help but consider the most central historical events and China's historical development in the context of Marxist philosophy.

Starting from 1949, the motive of democracy played an important role in China's history; it was introduced in China with the May 4th movement 1919, with Li Dazhao, an intellectual and theorist and China's first Marxist, while Chen Duxiu, who published the theory magazine "The New Youth" and led the May 4th movement's demonstrations, was the second most important promoter of Marxist theory and practice, leading to the foundation of the CCP and its broad popularization in the time of the CCP's and Guomindang's (further referred to as GMD) united front.

Let's take a look at the CCP, the party that led the successful revolution against the nationalist government, the GMD, in the first half of the 20th century, in order to understand its inner logic, collective and historic experience and traditions.

The discussion about democracy has played an important role throughout the history of the party, starting from the May 4th movement. The decisive event leading to the May 4th Movement of 1917, which lead to the establishment of the party, was the end of the First World War. In the peace conference in Versailles, China lost territory to Japan, even though the latter was among the losing powers. This provoked mass demonstrations in China's major cities. Chen Duxiu published a magazine, "The New Youth", which was created to overthrow the ancient system and rules in society and lift it onto a level internationally comparable with that of the materialistically developed nations of the 'first world'. 'Mr. Science' and 'Mr. Democracy' should play the crucial role in this process of national reorientation of a country which was not able to recover a leading place in the rank of capitalist countries, a position it held relatively to the Western countries until the first Opium War. Because of its unfair treatment by Western countries and consequently China's loss of territory, Chen lost faith in 'Wilson's ideas', the idea of equal treatment of nations, and orientated towards the Bolsheviks' revolutionary, Marxist, democratic and social (-ist) goals.

According to the theoretical principle of internationalism from below, the fate of the democratic revolution in Russia and the potential coming revolution in China and the whole world were closely connected. After Lenin passed away, the political character of the international, communist organization changed its revolutionary goals to a policy of class collaboration, i.e. in the Soviet Union and China the national bourgeoisie in both countries was taken as a political ally in the democratic revolution of the majority of people[7]. The CCP's strong orientation towards the Guomindang, pressed for until the bloody end by Stalinist strategists, ended up in a massacre of thousands of the communists by the nationalists in 1927 and the leadership of the CCP under Chen Duxiu was held responsible for the policy of orientation towards the nationalists forced upon Chen by Moscow. This was a huge setback for the whole worker's movement worldwide, a disorientation the Communist International answered globally with a reshuffle in national CCP leaderships. Two times the national leaderships were substituted in Germany and Great

---

[7] Wang Fanxi: Trotzki und der chinesische Kommunismus in Trotzki, Leo: Schriften 2, Über China, Band 2.1 (1924- 1928), p. 9-50, Rasch und Röhring Verlag, Hamburg, 1990

Britain, while other sections with a too critical attitude towards the wrong orientation were exchanged in Spain, Italy, Poland, France and China.[8] In the Soviet Union itself, the majority of the members of the party congress and the standing committee of 1934 and Soviet marshals were arrested and several thousand Red Army officers were shot or arrested, undoubtedly showing the shift in politics, followed by the necessity to remove elements of the old policy.[9]

The Soviet Union's leadership under Stalin gained a strong influence over the comparatively young and inexperienced movement in China. Even under the leadership of Chen, but more so under China's later Maoist leadership, the Soviet Union's Stalinist leadership was considered as its mentor and it had to maintain internationalist discipline. It was an important point of orientation for the People's Republic in all fields of society: policy, economy, education, philosophy, theory etc.

The Stalinist leadership had distanced itself from Lenin's way

---

[8] Grant, Ted: History of British Trotskysm, Well Red Books, London 2002, p. 17-24

[9] Sedov, Leon: The Red Book On the Moscow Trials, New Park Publications Ltd, London 1980, Chapter 1. online source: http://www.marxists.org/history/etol/writers/sedov/works/red/ch01.htm seen 18.02.2015

of handling political issues in theory and practice. The idea of democracy under Lenin aimed at bringing the international organization of communists all over the world to victory through national struggles of the proletariat against the bourgeoisie and imperialism. This idea was expressed in an international organization, a network, and the central organization which was supposed to unite and coordinate workers' representatives all over the world - the third communist International - was situated in Moscow. It became an expression of the shift in policy from Leninist to Stalinist, for example from an international orientation to a serving tool of Moscow's, i.e. Stalin's, interests. He subordinated the interests of the communist movement internationally to the national preferences of the Russian bureaucracy.

1.3. Mao's text "New Democracy"

Mao is the mastermind of the Chinese model of communism in China, a developing country. In the next chapters, I will refer to his key arguments and analysis. He keeps his criticisms in his writing "On New Democracy"[10] very general, direct, analytic and simple. Theoretically he clearly does not reach the level of a great philosopher like Karl Marx or Georg Friedrich Wilhelm Hegel, an influential philosopher who inspired a whole generation of philosophers, including Marx, though Mao's political visions are quite clear. He tries to apply a democratic model based on communism, developed by the European philosopher Karl Marx on Chinese conditions. A commune, the smallest unite of communism in a society, is basically a group of people working for a common present and future, and therefore they are sharing a common life by following a set of core principles. In Marx's view, these are decided on democratically by the commune. In history we see several examples of such primitive society, starting with the example of the commune of Paris that will be most central for our analysis, but also including the young Soviet Union as a positive point of reference. In Marx's communist model, all of the people rule in common and in solidarity, so there are no means of separation between nations or among individuals in

---

[10] Mao Zedong: On New Democracy, 1940, online source: www.marxists.org/reference/archive/mao/selected-works/volume-2/mswv2_26.htm, seen 08.2013

society. These means of separation today are for example racism, sexism, ethnic conflicts and, religious discrimination.

In Mao's writing "On New Democracy" we already realize the theoretical influence of the Soviet Union under Stalin. Moreover, in the 1930s translations of Marx were weak and not directly translated from German, but from German to Russian, to Japanese, and then to Chinese, which surely did not contribute to the quality of the outcome.

By the time he wrote it, in the first half of the 20th century, intellectuals, and especially communists in China as one tendency among them, were looking for a way "to change a China that is politically oppressed and economically exploited into a China that is politically free and economically prosperous"[11] and create a society that could move from the culture of ancient China to a new, enlightened and progressive one. Statements like these are purposefully vague , because the workers' movement at this time believed in the ability of people to organize their fate on their own and that the concrete process of democratization would take place in this process of

---

[11] Ibid.

self-empowerment of the people themselves. They believed that speculate on institutional reforms would be patronizing.

The spirit of these ideas has to be considered regarding their background. They were developed at a time when China as a nation struggled for survival against Japanese invasion, a fight that became part of the Second World War on one side, and a communist struggle against the nationalists, the GMD, on the other.

For the creation of a new culture in order to change humanity's social being, political and economic circumstances needed to be changed; however, according to Marxist philosophy, the economy is the fundament of society and politics are the concentrated expression of economy:

"It is not the consciousness of men that determines their being, but, on the contrary, their social being that determines their consciousness".[12]

Consequently, Mao saw the key to social change in the need to direct the revolution against the colonialists, i.e. foreign

---

[12] Ibid.

capitalism and the gradual growth of capitalist elements in Chinese society, brought about by these colonial powers.

The communists wanted to get rid of "the old colonial, semi-colonial and semi-feudal politics" [13] and the according economy and the culture brought about by ancient China and substitute them with a new kind of politics, economy and culture.

In this context, Mao already mentions a Chinese-style democracy, which would be new and special. He separated democracy and socialism by constructing the theory that China first had to transform the colonial, semi-colonial and semi-feudal state of its society into a democratic and independent society. In a further step, China could then build a socialist society.

Mao argued that, in the first stage, it was crucial for the proletariat and the farmers to make allies with the national petty bourgeoisie. This is a clear shift from the political line of Karl Marx who always promoted the independence of the

---

[13] Ibid.

proletarian movement, for example in the first international and numerous letters he wrote. This break with Marxist theory can be explained the following way:

First, China and Russia were both backward countries that did not have the relevant means of production, i.e. factories and industries before the revolution. Therefore, the proletariat was also not as developed as it was in 19th century England. The emancipation process was weak.

Secondly, shortage was a general phenomenon. Therefore, the generalization of shortage would and could not improve real democracy and emancipate people in China.

These two reasons contributed to the fact that China borrowed Stalin's Soviet policy model. Because the communist revolutions in Russia and China were isolated, the Stalinist government followed a policy of class collaboration and the Stalinist leaders equipped the working class of both the Soviet Union and China with the wrong tools for winning the fight against the bourgeoisie, which lead to the defeat of the proletarian movement in the cities in 1927, because of the betrayal of Jiang Jieshi, better known as Chang Kaishek, the leader of the nationalist party GMD.

Mao identified "the proletariat, the peasantry, the intelligentsia and other sections of the petty bourgeoisie" [14], with the proletariat as the leading force, as the determining, revolutionary classes in the bourgeois-democratic revolution, guaranteeing freedom of speech, assembly, press, voting etc.
After that, China could carry out the second stage of the revolution, where it would become part of a proletarian-socialist world revolution.
In his view, the European and American republics were (and according to Mao's criteria *are* even more so today) under bourgeois dictatorship. In contrast to these styles of democracy, China was going to be a democratic republic of another style, also essentially different from the USSR-style dictatorship of the proletariat. We can see him distance himself from already existing forms of state. He argues that revolutions in colonial and semi-colonial countries like China must adapt the form of a new-democratic republic, which is transitional, because it only suites a certain historical period, and constitutes republics

---

[14] Ibid.

under the joint dictatorship of *several* revolutionary classes, i.e. all anti- imperialist classes fighting the international bourgeoisie in the form of colonial powers. The CCP used "united front" tactics, i.e. a formation of several classes fighting for one common goal, to combine a bourgeois-democratic revolution with a socialist revolution.

In Mao's few, a socialist economy should be dominated by state enterprises, like banks, railways and airlines, which are operated and administered by the state, so a socialist character is guaranteed. These state enterprises shall not be completely financed by the state, but they can have state or private capital and the state will not confiscate capitalist private property generally and allow capitalist production, because the nation cannot survive on its own as the economy was relatively backward during Mao's living times.

The state could be seen as a pillar for the private sector, with the purpose of supporting it. Further on, the state economy would manage those sectors, which were too big to handle for a weakly developed Chinese capitalist economy that had not accumulated enough capital to make such huge investments in the 1940s, when Mao wrote these lines.

As Mao wrote in this central text, the CCP today sticks to his words, vowing to "never establish a capitalist society of the European-American type".[15]

In the first half of the 20th century, "capitalism was on the downgrade and socialism on the upgrade", and Mao identified it with a quote of Lenin as "the period of the final struggle of dying imperialism".[16]

Because of that, capitalist countries were even more dependent on colonies or semi-colonies, so they sought to avoid them establishing competing capitalist societies under the rule of their national bourgeoisie.

Mao stated, China should follow the principle of first fighting imperialism and feudalism, and during this fight introducing socialism.

In this situation, alliances were a tactical maneuver for the

---

[15] Ibid.
[16] Ibid.

communists, but, unless they were Stalin's orders, they had the purpose of developing a popular movement, and Mao only kept to alliances as long as it was necessary to build the organization, i.e. the party. History proved Mao's alliance policy in this situation and under these specific circumstances right, since he succeeded in conquering state power in 1949.

From the May 4th movement 1919 carried out by Chen Duxiu, Li Dazhao and other intellectuals and students, and the June 3rd movement, which took place one month later, Mao drew the lesson that an elite movement led by intellectuals could be strengthened when other classes, namely the proletariat, the urban petty bourgeoisie and, the national bourgeoisie and after the massacre especially the peasantry joined. At the same time, he realized the danger of bourgeois intellectuals - the right wing of the movement which converted to the side of the nationalists, the CCP's later enemies.

Those alliances, based on a broad class basis - the first and second popular front - he called the "united front". The alliance included workers and peasants, represented by the CP, as well as the petty bourgeoisie, represented by the GMD. In the first popular front, they successfully fought the warlords and united China. It ended for several reasons, one of which was that the right wing of the GMD crushed revolt (most notably in Shanghai 1927), leaving behind thousands of urban communists dead. As a result, the Communist International, located in Moscow, shifted its recruitment basis from the urban centers to the countryside. In the second popular front they had the goal of defending China against the Japanese army. The latter front only existed on a limited basis and was interrupted several times, and finally broke apart after Japan's defeat.

Only because of the ongoing war against Japan's invasion of China, the CCP could succeed in winning over power in 1949. In a backward country, primitive accumulation, i.e. the re-investing of capital for the development of society, was introduced and the means of production were created at a historically fast speed with extremely high rates of economic growth over a historically long period of time.

The concept of Mao's New Democracy was to create a nationwide culture with a socialist character that would reflect socialist politics and a socialist economy. True democracy is based on the conditions society provides. China's new, democratic culture would be closely connected with the world proletarian-socialist new culture as one part of human liberation.

New Democracy contains elements of a future, socialist society. It is not socialism yet, but a transformation stage in the fields of the leadership of the proletariat, politics, economy and culture. It uses a bourgeois-democratic revolution for combating imperialism and feudalism.

After finishing with imperialism and feudalism, and constituting New Democracy, the communist movement would have destroyed the main contradiction, the suppression by foreign powers and a backward economic system, and could concentrate on the establishment of communist ideas, Marxism-Leninism, i.e. communist theory and practice on a nationwide level.

After historically defeating feudalism, China got stuck between the bourgeois-democratic revolution and socialism. To use Mao's words, the old imperialism China faced from the first Opium war, until the declaration of the People's Republic, was substituted with a form of "new imperialism" after the Reform and Opening period by Deng Xiaoping after Mao passed away, which was a nationwide reform of the Socialist system and an opening up to foreign capital: Within the CCP, the national bourgeoisie's influence increased, while foreign capital was in a position strong enough to influence political decision making processes within the party. The national, as well as the international bourgeoisie, were limited in their attempt to gain control over the production process, the economic basis as well as policy making. We can see a very contradictory process: On the one side, influence by capital is wanted and needed as a way of a political system that lost connection to the masses and therefore tends to corruption and mismanagement, especially of big state owned enterprises (SOE), on the other side dominant fractions inside the CCP are very well aware of the danger of a too fast opening up process towards capitalism: it might destabilize the pillars of the policy making party for several reasons, as I will argue in my further analysis.

'Wholesale Westernization' was not an option in the path of the modernization process for Mao and is only represented by a minority inside the CCP until today. For the economy, an unlimited opening up to foreign capital would mean too much dependence on foreign capital and restrict the development of private capital in China and the power of the bureaucracy.

For popular education, Mao suggests to learning from the movement of the Enlightenment in capitalist countries. He was generally highly in favor of a broad and unorthodox education, including books like the Koran as a recommendation for a reading list of his niece for self-education.[17] He was very much in favor of universal education and was not at all dogmatic.

In order to handle information from outside of China, he gives a metaphor: It must be treated like "food - first chewing it, then submitting it to the working of the stomach and intestines with their juices and secretions, and separating it into nutriment to be absorbed and waste matter to be discarded before it can nourish us."[18]

We could generalize this order of action to the selective method of how China acquires non-socialist know-how, especially knowledge from abroad or traditional Chinese wisdom in

---

[17]   Feigon, Lee: Mao: A Reinterpretation, 2003, Ivan R. Dee, Chicago
[18]   Mao Zedong: On New Democracy, 1940, chapter 15: A national, scientific and mass culture. Online source: http://www.marxists.org/reference/archive/mao/selected-works/volume-2/mswv2_26.htm, seen 08.2013

general. However, today China does not fully stick to this plan. At universities, in the field of micro and macro-economics, economic theories are taught as they are in the West, sometimes even using the same English books.

To use it for our subject - elective democracy in China - can be very fruitful. There are mechanisms China could use very well from Western, elective democracies. Yet China has every right to be skeptical about adopting, for instance, the elective system of the US - a system that worked for ages already in the Western world, but tends to lose its legitimacy for developing countries, considering the financial and economic crisis, leading to a crisis of politics in the Western world today.

1.4. The CCP in Power

In the late 1950s, the Soviet Union and the People's Republic's cooperation suffered a severe theoretical conflict, ending up in the international isolation of China from its last ally among the super powers. This left China with no other choice than to build up the country on its own, based on its own strength, gradually mobilizing its huge population towards the task of isolated industrialization, without any foreign exports.

After Mao's death, his line was again gradually reversed by the economic faction in the Communist Party of China (CCP), through intelligent action de-facto but not formally headed by Deng Xiaoping, which consciously promoted an opening of the economy to the external world, including all its consequences; most importantly allowing capitalist market forces, i.e. the "invisible hand" the early liberal economist Adam Smith puts forward in the 18th century, to take control over extending parts of the national economy extensively. The years of relative international isolation ended gradually, the replaced by the economy-friendly wing of the bureaucracy. The Cultural Revolution was the famous movement that, in the eyes of most Chinese people then and today, shaped the modern China, but got out of the politicians hands. The introducing political campaign intended the destruction of old habits and traditions from the past in favor of cultural and industrial modernization and the implementation of radical democracy (as I argued in the previous chapter Mao's "New Democracy"). In the last years, out of two competing fractions, struggled for power, namely between the cultural revolutionary wing and the economically orientated wing. The latter won, with Deng Xiaoping on top, a top politician banned to the country side in the Mao era, who introduced the Reform and Opening policy in China, become China's paramount leader.[19] During his important inspection tour of the southern provinces in 1992 to convince all the comrades of the reform and opening policy, Deng Xiaoping stated, "If we do not adhere to socialism, do not implement the policies of reform and opening up to the outside world, do not develop the economy and raise the people's living standards, we will find ourselves in a blind alley."[20]

As a general idea that is valid until now, they maintained the state sector to keep limited control over the production process, but has been losing terrain relative to the private sector, even though the state sector has been growing.[21]

---

[19] Böke, Henning: Maoismus: China und die Linke - Bilanz und Perspektive, Schmetterling Verlag, Stuttgart, 2007

[20] "不坚持社会主义，不改革开放，不发展经济，不改善人民生活，只能是死路一条。"
关于《中共中央关于全面深化改革若干重大问题的决定》的说明，http://www.cnki.com.cn/Article/CJFDTotal-DJYJ201311006.htm, seen 09.2013.

[21] Wheatley, Alan: In China's economy as elsewhere, the state rises. Reuters Beijing Correspondant, 16.03.2009. online source: http://in.reuters.com/article/2009/03/16/idINIndia-38523620090316?

This sounds like a paradox, but this is possible because China's national economy is still growing rapidly today, so obviously this modernization strategy has been working in purely economic terms, not considering cultural or democratic development.

Since then, reformism, the gradual restoration of capitalism and the overwhelming concentration of power in the hands of bureaucracy without any democratic control, has become a phenomenon that endangers the people's democracy. It is done in the name of the defense of the revolution: The bureaucracy is afraid of the return of chaos and war as in the Cultural Revolution during Mao's rule, endangering the privileges of a caste that generally prefers stability. This is how the paradox of the balance between capitalism and rhetorical references to socialism are explained.[22]

----

sp=true, seen 11.09.2014

[22] Central Committee of the Communist Party of China (CCCCP): Explanatory Notes for the 'Decision of the CCCCP on Some Major Issues Concerning Comprehensively Deepening the Reform', China.org.cn, Beijing, 16.01.2014, http://www.china.org.cn/chinese/2014-01/16/content_31215162.htm seen 20.03.2014

2. Marx's Concept of Democracy

Generally, China's historical and theoretical development is described by the CCP the following way: Marxism-Leninism§, Mao Zedong Thought, Deng Xiaoping Theory and the thought of Three Represents by Jiang Zemin. It reaches from Karl Marx as the founder of scientific socialism (i.e. communism) to the most influential leaders of modern Chinese state philosophy. Specially, this thesis deals with the question of how far Marx's core theoretical ideas are recognizable in China's propaganda in the late Hu Jintao era, with the purpose of defining parallels and differences between Marx's democracy and the democracy of the CCP.

In various writings, Marx described his perception of history and his method. They changed and developed slightly in various aspects from his early writings to his later ones, so also the concept of democracy went through a kind of development. Let's first have a look at the beginning of Marx's perception of the concept.

In the 19th century, when talking about democracy most intellectuals had the connotation of democracy of ancient Greece, precisely of the Age of Pericles, which was in the mid-5th century B.C.E., in Athens. Marx's original idea and admiration for democracy was probably taken from this period. This argument is also supported by the fact that Marx wrote his dissertation after he changed from studying law to philosophy as his major, on "The Difference Between the Democritean and Epicurean Philosophy of Nature", dealing with the topic of freedom versus determinism in the context of Greek philosophy. The young Marx took an improved form of ancient Greek democracy as his ideal concept.

In ancient Greece citizens in assemblies resolved legal and executive matters, with the possibility for a delegation being sent to the Council of Five Hundreds, which was elected, as were the judges. Officials like tax collectors and generals were elected or chosen by lot. There was no need for a permanent, professional civil service, except for some lower-level functionaries. Self-exclusion from that process was socially despised; every male citizen was required to join the process.[23]

---

[23] Hunt, Alan: Marxism and Democracy, London: Lawrence & Wishart Ltd,

Unlike Hegel he discovered in his studies that no matter which theoretical concept aimed to improve society, no matter how precise the analysis was, concepts would not realize themselves by their mere existence. Just because one wishes for political change, it will not happen; change must be based on materialist change of the real world, i.e. of living conditions. Starting from the analysis of the present situation, a philosopher's task is to seek a realistic path for the improvement of society. Because the starting point of Marx's analysis is the majority of the population, he concentrates on the most advanced thinking elements of the majority of the population, the class of those dependent on selling their work - the proletariat. Marx calls Hegel's approach metaphysics and an ideology, because of his lack of this concrete method; Hegel's fundamental discovery led Marx to expand his search, opposing all metaphysics including that of Hegel, who he followed before. Marx developed his ideas on the basis of man's real life, i.e. practice, through the methods of historical and dialectical materialism. This is the revolutionary, methodological approach by Marx and Engels and used in their theoretical creation. Historical materialism includes the argument that historic events taking

---

1980, p. 76

place have patterns. Hegel, who originally introduced the method, points out that history, especially revolutions and social movements.

Dialectical materialism refers to contradictory processes. The thesis together with the antithesis forms a synthesis, for example: Political party A (thesis) and political party B (antithesis) form a coalition (synthesis), or the anger of factory worker (thesis) meets the arrogance of the factory owner (antithesis), so the solution of this situation is the occupation of the factory by the workers (synthesis).

These methods are an inherent part of Marx's thinking and therefore of this thesis. Today, several competing schools follow different interpretations of Marx's method of materialist dialectics. So the best point to start the search for a Marxist concept of democracy is with Marx himself.

2.1. Critics of Marx's Philosophy: Historic Materialism and Economism

Historically, Marx's philosophy starts from the inherent character of human beings, from its material analysis of their development, from their creation to the early stage of capitalism. Human practice, namely its relation to the external world, is the focus of Marx's philosophy, starting from man's interaction with nature to its adaption for his needs. Marx concludes, in his analysis of the history of human development, that human beings as a species are capable of creating a society, which is controlled and governed by the majority of the people, namely communism, a classless society.

Opponents often bring forward the fact that that Marx's philosophy merely focuses on economy and leaves out free will.[24] Concerning the criticism of the reduction of all reasoning to the basis of the economy, Frederick Engels, so to say Marx's soul mate concerning their radical philosophy of human liberation, states:

---

[24] One example would be: Rigby, S. H.: Marxism and history A critical introduction, 2nd edition 1998, Manchester University Press, Part One: Marx as a productive force determinist, p. 5-80

"According to the materialist conception of history, the ultimately determining element in history is the production and reproduction of real life. More than that neither Marx nor I have ever asserted. Hence if somebody twists this into saying that the economic element is the only determining one, he transforms that proposition into a meaningless abstract senseless phrase."[25]

The production and creation of the material world is changing our world. Work, including not merely wage work but also reproductive work, is the driving element for the development of society. The beings accomplishing and controlling the work process is the human species itself. These simple statements are the assumptions Marx and Engels built their theory on. Humans occupy most of their time with work, including different forms of work, such as wage labor, reproductive labor and the labor of subsistence agriculture in short, everything the human being does to secure his own and others' surviving, because modern-day humans are social beings within society and cannot survive alone in the long run.

---

[25] Engels to Bloch, Letter of 21/22 September 1890, online source: http://www.marxists.org/archive/harman/1986/xx/base-super.html#n14 seen 23.09.2014

"Men make their own history, but they do not make it as they please; they do not make it under self-selected circumstances, but under circumstances existing already, given and transmitted from the past."[26]

The development of consciousness for the determination of man's own history and to contrive ways and means in order to do so is the ultimate problem of the founders of scientific socialism, the communist system based on the analysis of Marx and Engel's life work and on the dynamic of true democracy from below. This model of true democracy takes a society system as a fundament that works according to a common plan, following the collective will of the people.[27] Hence, a democratically decided production process, or the control of the means of production by the workers and the people, is the basis for true democracy.

---

[26] Marx, Karl: The Eighteenth Brumaire of Louis Bonaparte. 1852, Chapter 1, online source: http://www.marxists.org/archive/marx/works/1852/18th-brumaire/ch01.htm seen 30.09.2014

[27] Engels to W. Borgius, Letter of 25 January 1894. in Marx Engels Werke 1968 (German Edition), Berlin, Vol. 39, p. 206; English online source: http://www.marxists.org/archive/marx/works/1894/letters/94_01_25.htm seen 15.01.2015

2.2. CCP and the Problem of Democratization

What would real democracy mean for the CCP and why are they against such an approach? They do not dare to shift power to the people, because they are afraid of the consequences, namely losing their privileges, which they have extensively accumulated since the Reform and Opening. In a reaction to people's request for democracy, the CCP tries to shift the attention of the debate to traditions of the past, in order to keep their power: Confucianism gets promoted again to legitimize hierarchy in society.

"The tradition of all dead generations weighs like a nightmare on the brains of the living. And just as they seem to be occupied with revolutionizing themselves and things, creating something that did not exist before, precisely in such epochs of revolutionary crisis they anxiously conjure up the spirits of the past to their service, borrowing from them names, battle slogans, and costumes in order to present this new scene in world history in time-honored disguise and borrowed language."[28]

---

[28]   Marx, Karl: The Eighteenth Brumaire of Louis Bonaparte. 1852,

Hierarchy in society is the exact contrary of the purpose of true democracy, which wants to dissolve bureaucracy within the population. In the following sections we will examine in detail and differentiate how and why the CCP holds up its position concerning true democracy in reference to Marx's approach.

The level of development is crucial for this article's equation of China's stage of development with the time Marx was living. In comparison with the US and Europe, the difference with the economic level in China is that the means of production are still relatively weakly developed and the primary sector (agriculture) still takes a big share of the total GDP, although the economy was for years and undergoes a rapid restructuring. Western scientists may consider the absolute numbers of factories, or people in the proletariat and consider is as a relatively large number of people. In fact, China's means of production are still weakly developed.

Chapter 1, online source:
http://www.marxists.org/archive/marx/works/1852/18th-brumaire/ch01.htm seen on 03.03.2014

Comparison of percentage of people employed in the primary sector (agriculture), secondary sector (industry) and tertiary sector (services)

	Germany 1882 [29]	China 2009	China 2013 [30]
Primary sector	41.6%	38.1%	31.4%
Secondary sector	34.8%	27.8%	30.1%
Tertiary sector	23.6%	34.1%	38.5%

We can see that both countries, even though temporally far apart, depend on a huge agricultural sector and have only a weakly developed industrial sector. This allows us to draw certain conclusions and consider problems of society, policy and democracy according to the method of historical materialism: Hegel argues that history repeats itself, even though it does so on different levels.

First we must define the frame of the discussion and delimitate it from today's Western discussion about democracy, which will be a side argument in the further text.

Marx admired the capitalist for breaking down the social relations to one decisive factor, namely pure capital relations:

---

[29] Sozialgeschichtliches Arbeitsbuch II. Materialien zur Statistik des Kaiserreichs 1870 – 1914, Vol. 2, p. 66, C.H. Beck Verlag, München, Germany, 1978

[30] 中国统计年鉴 2014, 中国统计出版社, 北京市 2015 年，四、就业和工资，就业基本情况
http://www.stats.gov.cn/tjsj/ndsj/2014/indexch.htm seen 16.02.2015

"The bourgeoisie, by the rapid improvement of all instruments of production, by the immensely facilitated means of communication, draws all, even the most barbarian, nations into civilization. The cheap prices of commodities are the heavy artillery with which it batters down all Chinese walls, with which it forces the barbarians' intensely obstinate hatred of foreigners to capitulate. It compels all nations, on pain of extinction, to adopt the bourgeois mode of production; it compels them to introduce what it calls civilization into their midst, i.e., to become bourgeois themselves. In one word, it creates a world after its own image."[31]

More detailed information about Marx' conception about democracy will follow in the chapter "Democracy and Marx" (chapter 4, p. 20).

---

[31]   Marx, Engels: Manifesto of the Communist Party. 1848, Chapter 1, online source: http://www.marxists.org/archive/marx/works/1848/communist-manifesto/ch01.htm seen on 03.03.2014

3. Research on the People's Daily

In the next chapter I will present the research about the Chinese conception of democracy.

After the economic crisis, China had already started to spend billions of Yuan on huge infrastructure projects, which were needed urgently. The world's biggest Keynesian program came along with a wave of new self- confidence in the CCP leadership, for their traditional anti-capitalist rhetoric, rooted in the Mao era, always stressed the vulnerability to any crisis of the Western, capitalist system. Hu Jintao was a member of China's top decision-making body, the Standing Committee of the Politburo, the General Secretary of the party, president of the state and Chairman of the military. From 2002 to 2012, he campaigned for more social justice, which was supposed to lead to equilibrium and harmony within society, this "harmonious society" was his program. During his time of reign, the income gap between the rich majority and the relatively poor majority of people empirically got bigger: Not only urban (17,175 yuan) and rural differences (5,153 yuan) grew.[32]

---

[32] Fu Jing: Urban-rural income gap widest since reform,

Regarding material injustice, even former premier Wen Jiabao warned in his final statement of office about the unbalanced state of society and economic development.

China's Gini coefficient's peak was 0.491 in 2008, 0.477 in 2011 and 0.474 in 2012, which is high for a country calling itself socialist. China has 2.7 million U.S. dollar millionaires and 251 billionaires, according to the Hurun Report, but 13 percent of its people live on less than $1.25 per day according to United Nations' data.[33]

This could lead us to the conclusion that the majority of people are excluded from the policy making process of wealth distribution and other decisions within society; that is to say, that the level of democracy, the rule of the people, stayed at a low level.

---

http://www.chinadaily.com.cn/china/2010-03/02/content_9521611.htm from 02.03.2010, seen on 10.10.2014

[33] Hornby, Lucy: China lets Gini out of the bottle; wide wealth gap, Reuters. Online source: http://www.reuters.com/article/2013/01/18/us-china-economy-income-gap-idUSBRE90H06L20130118 seen on 10.10.2014

3.1. The History of the People's Congress

The People's Congresses are a democratic system that might be described as a partly functioning relic of the Soviet Union. It has a nationwide, centralist state structure with basis groups. The system of People's Congresses, from the national level down to the district and township level guarantees all levels of society being able to elect representative governmental bodies onto the next level.

The National People's Congress (NPC) as the highest authority of China is the biggest institution of state power, deciding over political, legal, military and diplomatic issues on a macro basis. It is the largest parliamentary meeting worldwide, consisting of 2,987 members (2013)[34].

To completely gasp the current state and the system of People's Congresses in its transformation as a dynamic and changeable process, let us first of all have a look at the historical development of the idea of democratic centralism ideologically and geographically through the ages.

---

[34] China Internet Information Center, Beijing:
http://www.china.org.cn/english/archiveen/27743.htm and
http://www.china.org.cn/english/Political/26144.htm seen 10.05.2014

The theoretical basis of the People's Congress in China has traveled a long way from central Europe to China.

The discussion within the communist movement about the state structure of China, between Mao and those students returning from political university education in the Soviet Union, was won by the latter with the following consequence: The representative organs should have been similar to those of the Soviet Union. A Congress of Soviets should be based on regional and local soviets, according to the 1924 Soviet constitution. The bourgeoisie was explicitly excluded from election, while peasants were underrepresented relatively to their number in the population.[35] The "democratic centralism", as the theoretical concept the People's Congress was based on was called, is a centralist system, which came about through Lenin's improvement of the German theory of "social democracy", and was introduced to China after its adaption and generalization in the whole of the Soviet Union under a one party leadership.

The CCP is closely linked to the NPC and further has control over the composition of deputies, especially in the NPC. On lower levels, the procedure of pre-selection takes place in a

---

[35] O'Brien, Kevin J.: Reform without liberation: China's National People's Congresses and the politics of institutional change. New York: Cambridge University Press, 1990, p. 22

more decentralized way, and non-Communist candidates are tolerated, although the mode of elections keeps them from being elected for higher level assemblies. Between the regular annual meetings, the Standing Committee of the National People's Congress, containing around 150 members, is the constant representation of the NPC. Everyday business is handled by the Standing Committee of the NPC and, because of the dominance of the CCP members in the NPC, also exercises power over the Standing Committee. As a consequence, the representative organ, in theory controlled by the people, is in practice rather under the supervision of the party.

3.2. What is the People's Daily?

The People's Daily (人民日报 Renmin Ribao) is the most important, daily newspaper of the CCP in the one party system. This central publication follows a certain line given by the CCP - it is a strategic instrument with a purpose, directed by the CCP itself. In this way, it works as a channel of communication from the party to the masses of the people. We can consider this organ as an institution, which gathers information in society according to a certain, political and theoretical framework and serves as a tool to lead theory back to the people in order to become enrooted in society. The purpose is a specific selection of information, the embedding in a universal theoretical framework and the return to society, in order to influence people's practical behavior and lives. To follow this concrete task in service of the CCP, this organ is tightly organized. Unlike governing parties in Western countries, which keep a close, personal relation to the media in order to maintain political influence on the selection and presentation of information in the newspapers, the CCP directly controls the People's Daily and the People's Net (Renmin Wang), the online version of the newspaper, and can use the People's Daily directly to express their theory. Furthermore, it is not dependent on profit, but follows the task of propaganda. Therefore, as the biggest newspaper in direct control of the party, it has a unique position in society. The development of theory and its intermediation are highly standardized, compared with private or semi-private newspapers, and it follows a very concrete concept about what will be communicated and what won't.

Its main purpose is the publication of information in accordance with a narrative, controlled by the party, including questions of theory, governance, economy, culture, education, society etc.

The following research uses the digital collection of articles, published by the People's Daily on CD-Rom.[36] The articles with the term "democracy" in the headline were systematically put according to their most discussed content in the following graph, which shows the number of articles with each topic.

---

[36] Renmin Ribao 光盘版 电子版，北京，人民网版权所有. The archive of the years used between 2009-2011 is also available online: search.people.com.cn/rmw/GB/bkzzsearch/index.jsp

48

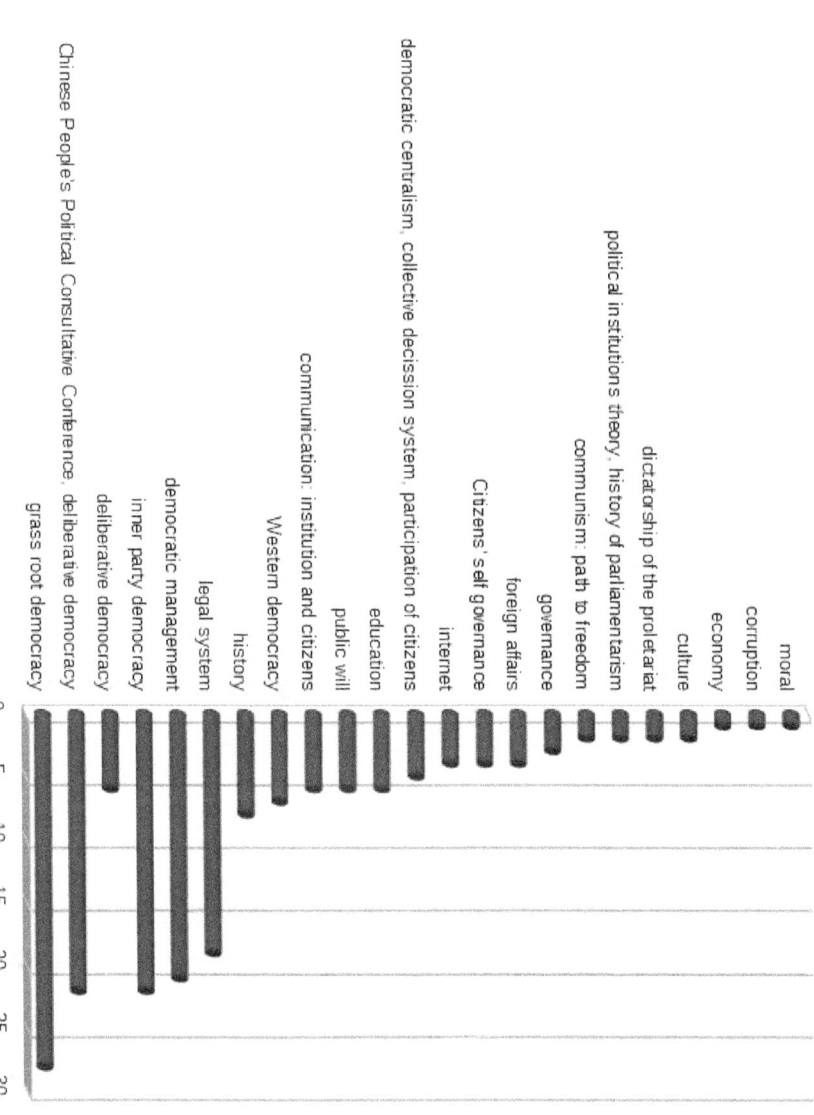

Chinese People's Political Consultative Conference, deliberative democracy, grass root democracy

deliberative democracy

inner party democracy

democratic management

legal system

history

Western democracy

communication, institution and citizens

public will

education

internet

democratic centralism, collective decission system, participation of citizens

Citizens' self governance

foreign affairs

governance

communism: path to freedom

political institutions theory, history of parliamentarism

dictatorship of the proletariat

culture

economy

corruption

moral

0   5   10   15   20   25   30

A general conclusion is that the frequency of topics varies in the years, although those articles were all published during the late Hu Jintao era. After the global financial and economic crises struck in the western world, China gained new self-confidence to find its own path instead of copying the well-approved capitalist path of the Western sphere. Even in the Western world, sales of Marx's "Capital" went up, people were looking for alternatives to the predominant Western capitalist system. So it is in China, where Marxist ideas might see a revival; for instance, central universities are ordered to put a strong focus on Marxist education of the students.[37]

On the following page, I will summarize the common content of the articles belonging to one topic. That way, we will get a feeling for what the democratic discourse in the given period is about.

Many different topics are referred to in one article, so the dominance of one topic in an article, according to which the research is designed, only gives us limited information about the relevance of that topic in the general debate, because one topic can play a minor role in most of the topics discussed. This

---

[37] Buckley, Chris: China Warns Against 'Western Values' in Imported Textbooks, The New York Times, 30.01.2015 http://sinosphere.blogs.nytimes.com/2015/01/30/china-warns-against-western-values-in-imported-textbooks/?_r=0 seen 10.02.2015

is part of the dialectical approach I chose; for example, morality is only the main subject in one of the articles analyzed, however, it plays a side role in most of the articles in the period the research focuses on. So, each topic will first be described shortly and in a second step the most relevant topics within the debate about democracy in China shall be dealt with.

Next, corruption and democracy are topics that are very closely connected to each other, although only one article is published by the CCP organ referring to this severe problem. It rarely appears as a side topic in the general discussion, perhaps because critics of a regime used to refer to it as a weakness. Throughout history, democratic movements have often protested against corruption, it might be described as a catalyst, a topic movements have criticized the regime for, whereby the suppressed and weak rebel against the strong. So corruption in connection with democracy is a topic hardly discussed, although corruption in general is a topic often discussed in society, and also in the People's Daily. The lack of a combination of the two topics in public debate might give a clue that the party wants to keep this discussion internal and give an example to the public about how deeply these topics may be discussed in public. The potential of real democracy to put an end to corruption is not mentioned.

The economy is, like morality, a topic which is rarely discussed in the Renmin Ribao (People's Daily) in connection with democracy, but which plays a huge role in the public legitimization of the government: The economic growth model has priority compared to questions like cultural plurality including minority languages or questions of climate, in short, to raise the average, material status of the masses is the party's mayor concern. Besides, often, phrases like "without the CCP, there would be no new China"; the picture of China the newspaper relates to is not the backward country China was in 1949, but the relatively economically rich and prosperous country it is now and it might become in the years to come. On the one hand, phrases like 'harmony' and 'unity' are also merged with the economy, for economic growth is an important criteria for stability, i.e. the content and therefore tolerance of the people for the CCP rule. On the other hand, economic failure will inevitably lead to a rise of contradictions within society and confrontation between the party and its people.

There is not much to say about the two articles that deal with culture and democracy. It plays a minor role in the discourse, though the CCP is committed to improve its cultural level. This will also only be possible in a better working, democratic system where minorities can improve their lives and live their different customs and traditions, as well as speak, study and improve local languages.

Although it has played a central role in history, the dictatorship of the proletariat is now a topic of almost no importance. It is sometimes mentioned as a legitimization in the Stalinist sense, namely, the CCP represents the proletariat and the peasants, and consequently its rule is just. The organ does not give any explanation as what this connection is, but it exists out of historic tradition. It was established by the party's founders, and because of their deeds, this connection, as it seems in the argumentation, is a natural and logical inference. In this Stalinist interpretation of Marx's philosophical heritage, the party does not need further legitimization or justification - the CCP leadership lives on the glory of the past generation of communists. The problem of a shift and eventually alienation from the legitimizing ideology does not occur, but a direct line of logic and natural development is drawn.

The <u>theory of political institutions</u> which express democracy and the <u>history of parliamentarism</u> are also put into the context of democracy.

<u>Communism as the path for freedom</u> is mentioned in two articles. It is one of few occasions where the officially ruling Marxist theory is interpreted as radically democratic, in favor of the liberation of human kind.

The system of <u>governance</u> is referred to in order to improve representatives' capabilities and the political system's functions - for example, the examination system - with the means of democratic participation, i.e. with deliberative democracy.

The democratic potential of the <u>Internet</u> is mentioned in only two articles. I want to add that this new technical innovation brought to humanity can be a powerful tool for debates in online forums, an exchange of ideas and the exposure of corruption, corruption and abuse of power. It creates a place for broad, public and open discussion, *although* this discussion is physically individualized and not collective: Information about body language, intonation etc. are not communicated through the written language which is mostly used on Internet forums and online chats. These are the mediums mostly used by activists who reveal such phenomena. Despite this disadvantage, the advantages predominate, given the purpose of the goal of a democratically planned society.

Another topic which plays a role in the debate is <u>citizen's self-governance</u>. Positive models of cities are presented where people managed to take city projects into their own hands.

The subject is closely connected to the topic of the collective decision system and the participation of the people in policy on the lower levels. These articles sometimes stress the positive role of democratic centralism.

The topic of <u>education</u> is discussed vividly: From the necessity of promoting talents and including them in the party as party members to recruit cadres, up to the necessity to raise the level of scientific democracy in decision making and the education on the countryside for peasants.

Research on the <u>people's will</u> (人民意志 renmin yizhi or short 民意 minyi) is a central focus in the context of democracy. According to this theory, representatives have to get to know people's opinions and interests and act according to them. We might imply that this mode of policy-making comes from China's ancient history, where emperors ruled with the legitimacy of not being overthrown: "While water can keep a boat afloat, it can also overturn it"[38] is an ancient, Chinese saying and refers to potential uprisings of the masses (water) and the danger of the government (boat is a metaphor for the ruler) to be overthrown. The good ruler qualifies through moral values and good will. According to this interpretation of good leadership, democracy does not describe the organic merger of state and people, but focuses on the separation of politics and production.

For good rule on each level, <u>communication between institutions and citizens</u> is of importance. Representatives improve their understanding of people's problems and can react accordingly.

Democracy was also important through <u>history</u>. Seven articles deal mainly with historical topics; portraying, for example, historical figures of the first half of the 20th century who held up the banner of democracy against critics. Another text deals with the new democratic revolution and has a more theoretical approach.

---

[38] 水能载舟，亦能覆舟 shui neng zai zhou, yi neng fu zhou

In the eight items focusing on Western democracy, the CCP makes the point that China will never introduce or copy the Western democratic model, focusing instead on improving a model of socialist democracy with Chinese characteristics. Obviously, the CCP seeks to rule out the possibility of Western lobbies expanding their political influence.

The debate about the legal system and the expansion of democracy and the rule of law (民主法治 minzhu fazhi). It is argued that people should be given the possibility to participate by law, and also that the right to vote must be improved (选举法 xuanjufa).

The important category of democratic management (民主管理 minzhu guanli) comes in line with the concept of people's will, the improvement of communications and the centralist political system: The bureaucracy on the lower levels should establish a practice of respecting people's interests and respecting them in their policies. Examples for articles dealing with democratic management are:
(1) a successful case in which citizens sued government representatives

(2) a public call for transparency of the finances for a city's public transportation system

(3) a conference between representatives of Chinese Buddhism and the party.

Again, this moral appeal as a recommendation is toothless, as long as the people cannot control the bureaucracy directly.

Inner party democracy is an important and very central tool for the party to improve democratic mechanisms. Because outer party democracy is weakly developed, inner party democracy is the only field where ordinary party members can engage with higher-level politicians and have an influence on the upper layer of deputies. The weak point of this system is that organizational structures are still too weakly developed to guarantee a vivid discussion forum of the people. The improvement of organizational structures and democratic consultations (民主生活会 minzhu shenghuo hui), literally translated as "democratic life assemblies" (meetings between citizens and political authorities or their representatives), are a focus for the authors of the articles. Once again, the lack of democracy, or power of basic members in relation to the top, blocks the development of real democracy, since high-level officials do not voluntarily improve institutions they are supervising or criticize them. Probably, this system of basic organizational structures help to keep up some connection of the top to the basis, i.e. basic democracy inside the party and have the potential to improve, but are more of a farce in the present stage.

28 articles deal with the topics of the "Chinese People's Political Consultative Conference", multi-party cooperation, deliberative democracy and elections. These are all categories where people or organizations, elements outside of the party, are consulted to become part of the party's internal decision making processes.

Two articles deal exclusively with elections, reporting on successful examples of such.

Six articles mainly deal with the topic of deliberative democracy, which was introduced only short time ago and is a very new topic in China. This concept is originally from Jürgen Habermas, a German sociologist and philosopher in the tradition of a pragmatic interpretation of critical theory. This deliberative democracy tries, according to the wishes of the CCP, to take people's will into account and reach a higher level of consensus. It compromises between the interests of the representatives and the people. Therefore deliberative democracy is not a model to promote true democracy according to Marxist philosophy, but rather has the role of stabilizing the CCP's rule and broadening its legitimacy. Even though it might be a topic of interest, I will not approach this topic in detail.

There exist several parties within the political system. Regular meetings on the so-called Chinese People's Political Consultative Conference between those democratic parties and the CCP take place at the same time as the National Congress. The problem with all the other parties besides the CCP is that these have a legitimacy to exist, but merely have a consulting function for the leadership and cannot make decisions. That means that party representatives can either accept the ideas of the parties and include them in their program, or reject them. A precondition for the allowance of these parties is that the leaderships of other parties must be loyal to the leadership of the CCP, so they have a harmonious relationship. There is no institutionalized hostile opposition standing up against the leadership of the CCP or its basic principles.

Considering the number of articles on the subject, the topic of grassroots democracy inside the CCP's institutions has the same, high importance as the previous subject. It deals with the bottom-up dynamics within the power structure behind closed doors. This central topic deals with, for example, bottom-up policy mechanisms, the problems of village party branches for the peasantry and self-management of peasants. Grassroots or "basis democracy" (基层民主 jiceng minzhu) carries within it the potential for emancipation, as it increases sovereign, communal circles of decision-making. Inside these potential structures of communes the people participating might make decisions for themselves.

Next, let's have a look at the content of the most central topics in the communication organ between the party and the people.

3.3. On Western Democracy

According to top officials, the development of democracy in China will not go in the direction of Western democracy, which several developing countries in Africa and South America or India copied. Several statements in the articles found in the People's Daily point in this direction, connected with different argumentation: "China cannot in any way introduce a Western multi-party system, and can in no way go the wrong way some developing countries did."[39]

The overwhelming majority of China's leadership and consequently most of the intellectuals state that the development of democracy in China will take a different path.

Western democratic systems are criticized as not being fully developed, which seems to imply that there are some mistakes. According to this theory, the Western, as well as the Chinese model of democracy, are still developing. Those kinds of Western models of democracy - with the state powers divided

---

[39] "我国决不能搞西方的多党制，决不能走一些发展中国家的错误道路" (独具特色的政治发展道路——如何理解"中国式民主" 2009.08.31.)

into legislative, executive, judicative - create situations where the different branches of government stand in the way of each other, because of different opinions about the same topic; while, in China, all the powers are generated by the People's Congress, and the People's Congress is responsible for them. Once a decision is made, there is nothing in the way of the plan being executed. Therefore, a law can be executed immediately.

The fact that policy-making can be a contradictory process with different laws, legislation or plans, opposing each other, is not mentioned, which might lead to the conclusion of an inappropriate approach about handling dialectical situations in society, even though such debates take place inside the party during the last years. Take the finance sector for example: While for the Industrial and Commercial Bank of China private capital was allowed to play a certain role, other big banks remain state owned as strategic key industries to keep up direct control of the state over the banking system. Similar processes we can see in the energy sector, where the coal industry is privatized, while the state owned industry invests in the renewable energy sector on a big scale. At least in this field we could conclude that the state seeks to keep up future orientated, strategic industries (renewable energy like wind, solar energy), while parting with coal power plants, i.e. energy forms with a negative effect on society and dying energy sectors in the long run.

We can conclude that the party keeps controversial debates to the inner party democracy mechanisms and does not want to carry it outside the party in public. This seems a mistake in so far that such central decisions affect the whole of society, so the whole nation should have the chance to take part in the debate, which is not given as I can judge from the research of the central publication and popularization organ of the party, the People's Daily newspaper.

Another problem is, that "Western electoral system often becomes money- dominating democracy and leads to social disintegration and conflict. The development of socialist democracy with Chinese characteristics must aim to guarantee that people have more practical democratic rights."[40]

This argument seems reasonable, considering the electoral system of the most developed country, the US, where candidates of top parties are heavily dependent on private donors to finance their election campaign. In this way, a state

---

[40] "西方的选举制度往往成为金钱支配的民主，导致社会分裂和冲突。发展中国特色社会主义民主，必须以保障人民享有更多更切实的民主权利为目标"
(在实践中坚持和发展中国特色社会主义民主; 颜晓峰, 2010.05.13.)

institution under direct control of the people could under certain conditions help to uphold people's control of state affairs. Marx describes the question about the character of a model for democratic control in his writings, for example on the Paris Commune.

In the context of democratic elections it says that the construction of "democracy is a gradual process, and 'gradual' does not mean it does not proceed, or proceed slowly or disorderly, 'gradual' should mean push forward actively and steadily"; a clear emphasis on the necessity for a push for democratic elections and participation of the people is very well made.[41]

In the eyes of the CP, basically, "democracy, as a civilized political system of human society, is always the ideal goal of the Chinese people, which has been diligently pursued for more than a century. But there are always two fundamentally different paths and modes about how to achieve democracy and

---

[41] "民主是个渐进的过程，但渐进不等于不进，不等于慢进，不等于乱进，渐进应该是积极稳妥地推进。" (选举法修正案草案提请十一届全国人大三次会议审议　选举法修改推进中国民主政治建设，毛磊，2010.03.09.)

realizing what kind of democracy" [42]. There are two points of view about the question of which characteristics a democratic process will have in practice: "The first one is to combine the fundamental principles of Marxism and China's reality to follow our own path and build the socialist democracy with Chinese characteristics; The other is to follow the way of complete Westernization and copy the Western capitalist democracy in China."[43] As mentioned above, the CCP decided to combine the principles of Marxism with "the concrete practice of China's revolution"[44], which, after all, followed the compulsion of an internationally isolated country. To further describe the historical background, the Communist Party of the Soviet Union after Lenin and under Stalin played the role of master for the Communist Party of China. The Communist Party of the Soviet Union passed on a political system to China, which was preparing for a course of isolation on a

---

[42] "民主作为人类社会一种文明的政治制度，百余年来一直是中国人民孜孜追求的理想目标。但对于如何实现民主、实现什么样的民主，始终存在着两种根本不同的道路和模式：一种是把马克思主义基本原理与中国实际相结合，走自己的路，建设中国特色社会主义民主；另一种是走全盘西化道路，把西方资本主义民主照搬到中国。中国共产党把马克思主义基本原理与中国革命的具体实践相结合" (中国特色社会主义民主政治的制度优势与基本特征—划清中国特色社会主义民主同西方资本主义民主的界限, 秋石, 2010.10.20.)

[43] Ibid.
[44] Ibid.

national level in the sense that the CCP was to serve the geopolitical interests of the Soviet Union rather than the goal of an international, proletarian revolution. One important political aspect remaining was the anti-imperialist orientation against international influence, i.e. the international bourgeoisie. The majority of the later generation of communists no longer followed an international perspective, with the purpose of freeing all people from suppression and establishing communism, according to Marx's interpretation. Along with this course of national isolation, a deformed revolutionary concept of democracy, namely a democracy for the people, not of the people, executed by a minority, i.e. a bureaucracy, was put into practice, both in the Soviet Union under Stalin's leadership, and, since China was an eager pupil of the Soviet Union, also in China under Mao's leadership, until the Sino-Soviet split of the late 1950s.

After the CCP came into power, "the Chinese people were led to overturn the rule of imperialism, feudalism and bureaucratic capitalism, established the state of people's democratic dictatorship with the workers- peasants alliance as the foundation, led by the working class" and "for the first time,

67

real people's democracy was established."[45] [46] Compared to the
monarchs of the past and the nationalist (Guomindang)
government, the communists presented themselves as the
progressive force for the people and democratic experiments
were carried out.

According to the national condition, these historical heritages
still exist today. "The CCP established the fundamental
political system and a series of specific political system such as
the system of People's Congress, the system of multi-party
cooperation and political consultation under the leadership of
the CCP, the system of regional ethnic autonomy, and the
system of community-level self-governance."[47] This political

[45] "领导中国人民推翻了帝国主义、封建主义和官僚资本主义的统治，
创建了工人阶级领导的工农联盟为基础的人民民主专政的国家，
在中国第一次实现了真正的人民民主" (ibid.)

[46] English source: CCCCP: Decision of the CCCCP on Some Major Issues
Concerning Comprehensively Deepening the Reform, Beijing,
China.org.cn, 2014.01.17, VIII. Strengthening Building of the Socialist
Democratic System, http://www.china.org.cn/chinese/2014-
01/17/content_31226494_8.htm seen on 19.05.2014
(Chinese source:中共中央关于全面深化改革若干重大问题的决定
（全文）八、加强社会主义民主政治制度建设 , online source:
http://www.china.com.cn/news/2013-11/15/content_30615132_4.htm
seen on 12.01.2015)

[47] "并从中国的具体国情出发，创立了人民代表大会制度、共产党领
导的多党合作和政治协商制度、民族区域自治制度、基层群众自
治制度等基本政治制度和一系列具体政治制度，找到了中国特色
社会主义政治发展道路，形成了与西方资本主义民主根本不同的

system of Socialism with Chinese characteristics is "fundamentally differently from Western capitalist democracy".[48]

An article in the People's Daily with the title "People's democracy is the lifeblood of socialism - Drawing a clear distinction between the socialist democracy with Chinese characteristics and the Western capitalist democracy" [49] gives a quotation of Hu Jintao, which argues that every political culture has a distinctive class character. Historically, he references the ancient Greeks and their city-state, where a very simple, but (especially in Marx's days, idealized) picture of democracy existed. In Chinese media, this model of democracy is criticized, with the argument that it was not really democratic because slaves, women and people from outside the polis were excluded from the 500 people, kind of plenary meeting, taking place in ancient Greece.

In the discourse, the "democracy with Chinese characteristics" will be formed according to China's own history. Even though

_____

政治模式。" (ibid.)

[48] Ibid.

[49] (人民民主是社会主义的生命——划清中国特色社会主义民主同西方资本主义民主的界限 , 2010.08.25)

a full development in the direction of Western democracy is excluded, China might still be prepared to profit from Western democratic systems to a certain extent.

> "For China indiscriminately imitating the system of Western democracy is a way not to be passed. (…) The established dictatorship after the victory of the "New Democratic Revolution" can only be the people's democratic dictatorship on the basis of the workers and its alliance with the peasant under the leadership of the workers; Accordingly, the state system and the political organization form can only be the democratic- centralist system of the People's Congresses." [50]

The CCP as the bureaucracy leading the country considers itself the vanguard of the people and is determined to seek political solutions *for* the people, its own political system.

Lenin's analysis about the Soviet Union mentions that bureaucracy would be abolished in the so-called "second stage of socialist society". Assigned to today's China, the goal for the Chinese communists would be such a "second stage of socialist

---

[50] "在中国照搬西方政治体制的模式是一条走不通的路。(...) 民主主义革命胜利后建立的政权，只能是工人阶级领导的、以工农联盟为基础的人民民主专政；同这一国体相适应的政权组织形式，只能是民主集中制的人民代表大会制度。" （李江源: 最符合我国国情的民主政治制度; 江西省邓小平理论和三个代表"重要思想研究中心教授, 2009.02.02.)

society". China's politicians point out that their political system should be as independent as possible from any Western system and therefore Western influence, because they assume that a political system closer to the Western one tends to be more liable to foreign domination.

In order to keep up independence from Western power, the CCP follows the task of developing its own methods, guaranteeing a certain degree of democratic development.

> "One important aspect for the development of a democratic policy is to develop people's democratic consciousness and their democratic ideas and to raise the people's democratic disposition."[51]

Hence, there is a commitment to the term democracy, the participation of the people in discussions, which is second-rank and led by a minority inside the party. The fact that the issue of democracy is discussed reflects the relevance of this topic for society; it cannot simply be ignored, even under sensitive political circumstances.

---

[51] "发展社会主义民主政治，一个重要方面就是培养人民群众的民主意识和民主观念，提高人民群众的民主素质。" (发挥网络文化在发展民主政治中的作用, 宋元林, 2009.04.08.)

The discussion about the character of democracy with Chinese characteristics could be described as "harmonious", namely because it avoids the topic of mass incidents or violence on the theoretical level. Also when choosing which kind of topics to adopt from Western democracy, the leadership rather chooses the concept of deliberative democracy, which fits the concept of the harmonious society, a key ideological phrase in the era Hu Jintao, in the following way: It describes a model which ideally solves contradictions through consultations among actors, for example the bureaucracy, representatives of a factory and the people, assuming that class differences about common interests of a group can be dealt with among equal partners and can be solved through negotiation. The method of consultation is just to balance both sides' interests and to make policy as far as possible according to the appeal of the majority. Marx comments that under bureaucracy, man as the subject becomes the object of manipulation.

We can see the idea of 'equilibrium within society', which can be brought about through negotiation, excluding power structures, economic pressure and other factors.

CCP intellectuals claim that there is a mistake in the conception of the model of Western democracy: In the US, Europe and elsewhere in the world, Western democracy turned into a strategy for politicians and their clique to stay in office (a critique which seems true for the overwhelming majority of governments in every system all over history, including the CCP). The attitude in Western politics is, according to the People's Daily, as long as the system is good, it does not matter who is in charge.[52] This would simply have the consequence that the system won't work anymore, because there is no strong figure to step in and step in for the people to solve society's problems any more. The system perpetuates itself, including those in power.

The problem of the Western policy system today is that it works on its own stability rather than on society's functionality and most important problems, which tends to lead to crisis. This problem, the CCP intellectuals name, is mentioned by Karl Marx as the vulnerability to crisis of capitalism. Marx analyzed it with the theory of capital accumulation and the tendency of the rate of profit to fall. Because of the corrupted politicians, standing in the service of capitalists rather than the voter, the crisis we face today is exact such a crisis: The bubble in the real estate sector is caused in speculation in non-

---

[52]   发挥网络文化在发展民主政治中的作用, 宋元林, 2009.04.08.

productive sectors rather than industry, consequently the breakdown of part of the banking system, part of the real economy follows: companies breaking down, and even more, so the argument of the very same article mentioned above, the army might not be capable of fighting anymore and the system might break down completely, all due to the corrupted governments in Western countries.

At the same time, so the argument, capital's influence on democracy is gradually rising, especially in the U.S. where Barak Obama received huge support from Wall Street for his first election campaign and an immense sum of tax payer's money was used to save the national economy and the banking system at the beginning of the economic crisis. One of the co-authors, a Marxist, sharply criticizes the system of Western parliamentarism and says that the contradictions between the capitalists as a class and the pressure from below might overwhelm neo-liberal and Keynesian ideology and lead the way to socialism.[53]

This seems to be a quite profound analysis in the tradition of Marx's analytic style, although it is one of view exceptions among all the material analyzed.

---

[53] 张维为　曲星　程恩富　沈丁立：高祖贵透视美欧制度性问题——"钱主"左右"民主"会带来什么？, 2011.12.22.

3.4. From Theory to Practice

Although the CCP states very clearly that it opposes Western democracy, it has not yet developed an alternative path to socialist democracy in practice. There are hardly practical examples that fit the line about rhetorical enthusiasm of the slogan "people being masters of their own affairs", throughout the newspaper. The vision of what socialist democracy could mean in practice is rather vague, although examples of elections are mentioned. One article concerning the interaction between urban planning and democracy mentions that, "projects, concerning people's lives, are carried out in a democratic way".

In Ninghai, a city with about 600,000 inhabitants in Zhejiang province, representatives of the People's Congress conducted studies about which infrastructures were needed to be built in the city. People were questioned about which projects were needed most desperately. The survey decided on the building of a professional track inside a school, since students formerly had to go jogging outside the school for their gym classes. On the one hand, this might seems a very modest example of democratic management, on the other hand these steps are linked with the demand for the realization of "scientific and democratic policy": people rejoin control of the implementation of project, but the purpose of these requests is that, as suggested in the article, "People's projects are carried out in a democratic way", to "dissolve social contradictions on a grass root level", serving the purpose of a harmonious, stable society. [54]

In this case, we can see attempts of the party organ to realize a very primitive kind of democracy in practice on a local, easy to control level, which shows some potential to be generalized. Because of the decentralized structure of the policy making process, experiences concerning policy reforms in general, including experiences with democratic reforms, first have to show their success on a local level. Only after it is proven that they work, can they then be slowly extended. It usually takes decades from a change in policy on a local level to its extension to a nationwide policy.

It's a process to slowly establish the essential skills which are necessary to get familiar with those mechanisms for the improvement of the Chinese system, concerning for instance the one child policy, which is scattered in some regions, or

[54]   裴智勇：政府工程由人大代表票决　宁海：民生工程走民主程序, 2010.04.14.

capitalist mechanisms, which were implemented from the 80's onwards and are now an integral component over-weighting the former state sector. The process works by the experts in central government first analyzing the experiences for example from various self-government regions; only afterwards can it be decided on whether to generalize the knowledge drawn from the conclusion, and if it serves the purpose of the central government - in short, if the introduction of a certain policy is beneficial to society from the view of the government or if it might be harmful. We can assume that the central government is often rather skeptical about flattening down hierarchic structures of mechanisms of government due to central functionaries' fear about loss of control.

We can recognize a slow process, in which the official line of argumentation is to promote democracy in theory, even though doubts exist about the introduction of democracy, of bureaucrats involved blocking and sabotaging the reform process. In this way, participation of the people is only allowed as long as it does not contradict the interests of the party bureaucracy, while constructive critical comments are sometimes tolerated.

After the founding of the Republic in 1949, China's economic development, and with it the overall development process of society, began from a very low stage. The majority of the population was rural in terms of class affiliation. On the other hand, capital, and along with it the means of production and workers, was hardly concentrated in urban centers due to the low development level of capitalism in China on a general basis. Hence, the economic foundation assumed by Marx for a democratic development, the working class, was hardly existent, which led to theoretical and practical problems about the introduction of communism.

The idea of the "New Democratic Revolution" describes an evolutionary concept, according to which the new democratic revolution must first be concluded before the preconditions for the redirection of the revolution towards socialism is given. In other words, assuming that socialism is the system, where the working class can fulfill its task of controlling the means of production and execute its will in a direct, democratic way, socialism cannot yet be reached until after the conclusion of the "New Democratic Revolution". Hence, the realization of socialism and real democracy with the working class as its main pillar becomes a task for the future, rather than a task of the present. In other words, the CCP has not laid its foundation and its class basis on the working class up to now, even though it states it has:

"The working class is China's most progressive, most revolutionary and best organized class, and the natural leading class of China's democratic revolution. Consequently, the democratic revolution of China can only be the 'New Democratic Revolution' under the leadership of the proletariat. The CCP, as the vanguard of the proletariat, becomes of couse the leader of the new, democratic revolution. (...) The proletariat as the leading class and the CCP as the leader inevitably will, after the conclusion of the new democratic revolution, lead the revolution in the socialist direction."[55]

Furthermore, a new bourgeoisie came into existence after the introduction of the 'Reform and Opening' policy, even though a certain group inside the CCP seems to be aware of the dangers of its own national bourgeoisie and its harmful role in

---

[55] "工人阶级是中国最先进、最革命、最有组织性的阶级，是中国民主革命的天然领导阶级。因此，中国的民主革命只能是无产阶级领导的新民主主义革命。中国共产党作为无产阶级先锋队，理所当然地成为新民主主义革命的领导者。(...) 无产阶级作为领导阶级、中国共产党作为领导者，在完成新民主主义革命后，必然要把这一革命引向社会主义方向。" (中华民族伟大复兴的必由之路——为什么只有社会主义才能救中国，只有中国特色社会主义才能发展中国，而不能搞民主社会主义和资本主义, 综合, 2009.06.03)

the development of socialism, according to its own, reformist path.

> "The national bourgeoisie has a strong desire to develop capitalist economy, but it doesn't have the courage or the ability to completely overthrow imperialism and feudalism, since it is inextricably linked to them."[56]

The workers' interest is their own emancipation, the control of the means of production to create a human world according to their needs, while the national and international bourgeoisie's interest is the exact opposite, to control the means of production in a capitalist manner, on behalf of the workers, suppress them in their economic and cultural development by taking their profits for their own purpose. We can see that the interests of proletariat and bourgeoisie are diametrically opposed. The national bourgeoisie is very much in favor of the development of capitalist economy and due to its links with dependence of international capital it cannot just overthrow imperialism and feudalism, which is necessary as a precondition to establish worker's control and real democracy.

---

[56] "民族资产阶级有发展资本主义经济的强烈愿望，但由于与帝国主义和封建主义有着千丝万缕的联系，没有彻底的反帝反封建的勇气和能力" (ibd.)

Instead, the CCP legitimizes its rule and leadership on behalf of the people historically and therefore states that democracy with Chinese characteristics

"is people's democracy led by the Communist Party of China. Without the CCP, there would be no new China [China after 1949 under Mao, note], there would be no people's democracy, that's an objective fact, proven by history. The Chinese people are masters of their own affairs, this was achieved by the CCP through an extraordinarily difficult fight."[57]

The leadership of the CCP, as the successors of the revolutionary power of the first half of the 20th century, defines itself as the deputies of the people, however they are in fact a ruling bureaucracy on behalf of the people; while claiming to uphold the rule *of* the people, the CCP and all its structures represent a rule *for* the people. The political caste defines democracy as an important mechanism to balance between the government's and society's satisfaction.[58] Democracy in its

---

57 "它是中国共产党领导的人民民主。没有中国共产党，就没有新中国，也就没有人民民主，这是被历史证明了的客观事实。中国人民当家作主，是在中国共产党领导下经过艰苦卓绝的斗争实现的。" (独具特色的政治发展道路——如何理解"中国式民主"，2009.08.31)

58 民主就是一种权衡"政府满意"与"社会满意"之间的重要机制; 民主

original sense basically means 'rule of the people'; in the Chinese context, the party is an intermediary in between the people and state control in society, an intermediary with a purpose, only partly dependent on the people's approval and the people's will.

是一种纠错机制, 张洋 (2011.08.24)

3.5. The Role of Democracy for the Party and inner Party Democracy

China claims that Western countries, especially the U.S. and Europe judge over the very definition of democracy. Common values within a nation, such as freedom, the rule of law and human rights are upheld, whereby Western democracy is used as a scale to divide the nations into two categories, namely democratic or undemocratic. First, the idea of democracy went through historical changes over time. In the ancient Greek metropolis, only male inhabitants could vote, while females were excluded. Immigrants to the metropolis or slaves were excluded from the right to vote too. Even in the European age of enlightenment, the intellectual discussion about self-empowerment of the people took place, while during slave trading in Africa to America, two thirds of the slaves died.

Even today, immigrants cannot vote for years in most countries.

The debate always takes place under certain aspects, but is developing over time. Through the fight of suppressed nations for sovereignty and the international prohibition of slavery since the early modern age, the circumstances for the discussion of the topic have changed.

Nowadays, the CCP agrees that democracy has, as a controlled way of expression, a very positive effect on society as a whole and guarantees stability if expressed through controlled channels, under the supervision of the CP. The introduction of democracy in China can help "to realize the extensive people's democracy, to flock together the huge wisdom and ability of the people and to establish national long-term, stable development"[59] and therefore has very positive effects on the balance of class forces.

The party works on reforms of the democratic system and "the most important way for the party to carry out the concept of democratic governance is to develop inner-party democracy", namely "to guarantee the democratic rights of party members, improving the party's congress system, give full play to the function of plenary party committee session, reforming the inner-party election system, and improving the inner-party supervision system", whereby the improvement of the congress

---

[59] "实现最广泛的人民民主，汇聚最广大人民的智慧和力量，国家长期稳定发展" (ibid.) and (民主之花　精彩绽放, 李章军, 2010.03.06.)

system has the highest priority. Congresses at all levels and the committees elected by them are the highest bodies of the party.[60]

The People's Congresses, representing state power, are present at all five levels: national, provincial, municipal, country and township level. The deputies for People's Congresses at both the country and the township level are directly elected. However, the candidates need to be approved by the party.

This constitutional democracy is based on the framework given by the constitution and refers to the People's Congresses. Theoretically, people exercise state power through the regional people's congresses by law and the National People's Congress as the highest authority of the national, democratic system. The congresses are "responsible for the people and should be supervised by the people. National administrative organs, judicial organs and procuratorical organs are elected by the People's Congress" and supervise it.[61]

---

[60] Liu Jianfei (刘建飞): Democracy and China, New World Press 2011, Beijing, p. 44-53

[61] Ibid.; The so-called Supreme People's Procuratorate (最高人民检察院 zuigao renmin jianchayuan) is one institution in the People's Republic of China , an agency for prosecution and investigation. Hong Kong and Macau are influenced by the legal traditions of former imperialist, Western powers (for Hong Kong: Great Britain; for Macau: Portugal),

The term of all people's congresses lasts five years, the National People's Congress takes place once a year, while local people's congresses should be held at least once a year according to the constitution, and every bill drafted by the congress is examined by experts and assessment meetings.

The people's congresses fulfill the function of legislation - supervision, appointment and dismissal - and decide about important events and guarantee the people to be masters of the country – at least in theory.

Practical problems are that concerning representation, workers, peasants and especially migrant workers, who make up the majority of the population, are hardly represented in the highest institution, the National People's Congress.

So inner party democracy, the democratic rights of CCP members and democratic mechanisms are, together with the People's Congresses, the most important, institutionalized pillars of the democratic system in China, according to the definition of CCP authors. Additionally, multi-party

---

accordingly their legal system resembles the one of the old, colonial powers, i.e. rather follows the general character of Western legal systems.

cooperation provides institutionalized consultation by some parties, under the leadership of the party.

For the deputies of those congresses it's hard to live up to their formal expectation of taking responsibility on behalf of the people and controlling the state affairs for them, because people's congresses normally only take place once a year and there is no other effective way to do their duties; often they become merely a formality of inspections of laws and other legal issues.

In specialized Chinese literature, there is an example of Shangcheng district in Hangzhou, Multicipality: The people didn't know the deputies of their neighborhood, district, municipality or province. Deputies did not feel a strong responsibility towards the people. Therefore, people encountering problems relevant for the deputies to improve the city's policy did not turn to the deputies. As a reaction, the district installed a model system for the people to meet the deputies at all levels directly every two months.[62] This meeting might help to improve the connection between people and the representatives and improve the latter's policy making.

---

[62] Liu Jianfei (刘建飞): Democracy and China, New World Press 2011, Beijing, p.48

In the People's Daily, there is a strong focus on leading together inner party democracy and the development of grassroots democracy, which finds its expression in the rising number of publications of articles in the newspaper, starting in the year 2010. The leadership has an interest to be closer linked to the people as such and it wants to strengthen this connection, both within the party structure and in the state structure, which are officially not linked to each other.

The inner party democracy is one of the most important argument for the existence of democracy in China as such in this discourse, and the overlapping of inner party democracy with grassroots democracy carries along a strong potential: "The starting point and the fulcrum for the construction of democracy are people at the grassroots."[63]

The CCP describes itself as a "huge party with more than 370.000 organization groups on the basic level and more than 77 million members" and asks the question of "how to handle the relation between 'top down' and 'bottom up' in a good way, as well as how to push forward inner party democracy and the development of people's democracy by inner party democracy at the grassroots level?"[64]

---

[63] 基层是民主建设起点和支点, 许耀桐, 2010.07.08

[64] "一个有 370 多万个基层党组织、7700 多万名党员的大党 如何处理

The number of members and the at least rhetorical willingness for reforms in connection with democracy is a testament to the relevance of the discourse of the mass party on society. An institution as big as that is an important factor for the development of consciousness in society and we can see the CCP asks the right questions, though on an abstract, theoretical level. However, we cannot assume that all of these 77 million members are active and organized in one of the 370,000 organizations, where heated or controversial discussions take place about relevant topics, from the participants' daily problems to the future of the nation. These might be the case in some groups, especially on higher levels, but it is not a general phenomenon.

According to the number from the end of 2012, out of the then 85.13 million party members (6.3% of the total population is organized in the CP), only 7.25 million or under 10%, were workers. This is a rather low percentage for a party which claims to exercise power on the basis of a peasant-worker's alliance under the leadership of the workers, whereby the

---

好"自上而下"和"自下而上"的关系，以党内基层民主推动党内民主和人民民主的发展？" (党内基层民主实践案例, 2010.07.08.)

people are masters of their own affairs, as repeatedly stated in the material investigated in the study on the People's Daily. [65]

The fact that in the year 2012 more "than 44 percent of new members are frontline workers, such as industrial employees, farmers, herders and migrant staff" joined the party suggests that the CCP realized this symptom of deformation and the lack of a class basis, so there have been moderate changes in the priority of recruitment according to underprivileged groups.

The official argumentation indicates that the CP, with its historical legacy and relying on the state-structure of one party rule, acts as a judge over the legitimacy of mechanisms of democracy and claims a monopoly over the discussion process. This opinion is supported by the statement, the "overwhelming number of party carders live among the masses"[66], however this concerns only the basis of the CCP members, whose influence on the decision-making process is limited. Those

---

[65] Xinhua: China's Communist Party membership exceeds 85 million, Xinhua, Beijing, 01.07.2013., http://english.CCP.people.com.cn/206972/206974/8305636.html seen 25.05.2014

[66] "广大党员都生活在人民群众之中" (李江源: 最符合我国国情的民主政治制度; 江西省邓小平理论和"三个代表"重要思想研究中心教授; 2009.02.02.)

members at the upper levels have no close link to the working class. On the contrary, part of the working class feel alienated from leading party members because of material, financial and social privileges they are granted, which are considered as unequal treatment by the workers.

We can experience a willingness to expand 'bottom up' mechanisms. In rural and minority areas, autonomous regions have limited rights for self-governance.

"The mass autonomous system is only one part of the construction of democracy, a broad variety of the people on the grassroots level's self-governmental practice offer important experiences for the construction of inner party democracy and inner party democracy's development, and the development of inner party democracies will inevitably be an important example and motivation for the people's democracy within people's grass root self-governance."[67] So these areas offer supply for know-how and skills of self-governance practices to the party and for its purposes. At the same time, a command for standardization can be interpreted in the words "will inevitably

---

[67]　"群众自治制度并非是我国民主建设的"独角戏"，丰富多彩的基层群众自治实践为党内民主建设提供了重要借鉴，而党内民主的发展，必将对包括基层群众自治在内的人民民主产生重要的示范和带动作用" (民主政治的生动课堂, 廖文根, 2009.10.28.)

be an important example and motivation for the people's democracy within people's grassroots self-governance". Hence, people's democracy has to be a part of the whole system and cannot detach from it. These are the top-down limitations for the development of people's democracy.

The People's Congress, as the highest level of the state structure, also "helps to perfect the leadership system of the party, improve inner party democracy, and avoid over-concentration of power"[68].

The few articles in the context of ethnic minorities focus on economy and development, while the word harmony, the typical, ideological Hu Jintao construction of peaceful coexistence without class struggle, is frequently used.[69] Conflicts in Tibet 2008 and especially still ongoing ones in Xinjiang are extremely severe, while in Yunnan, the province with the most pluralistic groups of minorities, the coexistence between Han Chinese and the minority population (which makes up the majority in many villages in Yunnan) seems to work fine according to the CCP's plans of economic

---

[68]   "有助于完善党的领导制度，发展党内民主，避免权力过分集中" (ibid.)

[69]   建立民主管理 振兴民族产业 (综合), 2011.08.19

development. "Economic democracy"[70] is another term to be found in Chinese special literature. In the Western understanding, economy and democracy are not linked to each other, but are different concepts, although economy plays a role in the question of a revolution by Marx: Only if a system cannot improve the material needs of its population any more, it *can* be substituted. It will only be substituted if there is a strong people's movement which can take over power of the weak government, which cannot fulfill the materialistic needs of society anymore and holds back people from developing their lives as they want and need. So "economic democracy" in a Marxist sense can be understood as the interaction between the people and the government, based on economic factors: If the economy is developing well and people can raise their living standards, the system works. In case economic growth weakens and the capitalists want to improve their profits, the base for a growth of people's living standards is not given any more. So if workers feel a huge level of exploitation - the discrepancy between the work done and the material benefit they get back from a society controlled by representatives of capitalists - then the economic balance is uneven and people will shout for justice. This might develop up to the point when

---

[70]   Liu Jianfei, Democracy and China; New World Press 2011, Beijing, p. 31-44

the working class successfully substitutes the old state apparatus with a new one, and dissolves it to abolish all class contradictions.

Another concept is grassroots democracy. In the Chinese context it describes a form of organization in urban and rural residential areas, as well as in enterprises, and consists of committees or workers' congresses, which act under the leadership of the party. "The realization of people's self-governance system on the primary level, i.e. the implementation of self-management, self-service, self-education, self-control (...), includes the basic people's self-governance system with rural villagers committee, cities neighborhood committee and enterprises employees' representatives' conferences as its fundamental program."[71]

There are various organizations on the primary level. By the end of 2012, the party claims 4.2 million party organs in 33,000 towns and 588,000 communities.

In these organizations it's not clear how far they are dominated

---

[71] "实行自我管理、自我服务、自我教育、自我监督的基层群众自治制度(...)包括以农村村民委员会、城市居民委员会、企业职工代表大会为主要内容的基层群众自治体系。" (符合国情的社会主义民主政治模式, 翁杰明, 2009.06.08)

by a bottom-up, or rather a top down character, to what extent the people can vote for deputies or the possibility to vote a deputy out, which Marx analyzed in the Paris Commune. Apparently, the election process does not take place independently; the local government can pre-elect candidates and take control over certain decisions. Apparently, the pre-election mechanism does not work democratically at all, as one article proposes the improvement of pre-selection mechanisms for candidates.[72] Every Chinese person knows that such a formulation means that there are still severe problems. Though, the topic of elections gains increasing importance in the debate.

For example, the People's Daily states that contradictions among the US, China and South West Asia shall be handled in a democratic way. Through the theory of Marxism, applied in the concrete practice of the establishment of democracy in China, 1.3 billion Chinese have an unprecedented potential to be masters in their own house against the old aggressors in the 19th and the beginning of the 20th century.[73]

China is not dominated by Western powers and Japan as it was

---

[72] 盛若蔚: 坚持民主公开竞争择优用人方针，坚持注重基层的用人导向抓住换届时机　配强党政正职, 2011.07.26

[73] 王恬　张晓　黄培昭　李潇: 鼓励相关国家向民主过渡，支持巴在1967年前边界内　建国　美国西亚北非　政策调整引争议, 2011.05.21

the case as a consequence with the opium wars 1839-1842 and 1856-1860. Nowadays, China as a nation (not talking about domestic policy) gained it's sovereignty back today, however "true democracy", or people's democracy, has not been developed yet, although the government has the power to do so, if they relied on a real Marxist program.

On a local level, there are very well competing candidates allowed for elections at the bottom end of the governmental hierarchy, but this does not automatically conclude in a debate of participants with equal rights. Within the given framework, deputies can only discuss everyday problems and are not allowed to critically discuss systematic problems and big changes within the political system. Given the existing limitations, democratic dynamics cannot emerge. The systemic flexibility necessary for real democratic mechanisms is not given. The one party system, which makes the discussion processes easier to control, concentrates power and control of systematic questions high up at the top end of the state and, more importantly, party institutions; as a result, despite all the rhetorical willingness for reforms and improvement, at this point, democratic mechanisms don't work too well.

3.6. Legislation

Historically, China hardly has a sophisticated system of law. According to the trend of a learning effect from the Western system in this sector, projects regarding the development of the 'rule of law' are advancing, even though they still are at a low stage. The creation of a practical and operating legal framework is linked with the debate about equality.

> "Equal rights are fundamental rights of citizens, but also one of the essence of the rule of law in the country. Draft amendments to the electoral law, which uphold the concept of human equality, area equality and ethnic equality all made a substantial progress in the course to Chinese democratic politics." [74]

In the CCP's point of view, democratic centralism is the highest form of democracy, which has an advantage over capitalist democracy:

> "The power structure represents that the legislative power of the

---

[74] "平等权是公民的基本权利，同时也是法治国家的精髓之一。这次选举法修正草案，秉持人人平等、地区平等、民族平等的理念，在中国民主政治进程中迈出了实质性的一大步。" (选举法修改，同票同权扩大人民民主, 谢卫群, 倪光辉, 刘维涛 , 2010.03.14)

people's will exceed the executive power and the judicial power, which forms democratic centralism, China's People's Congress is just such a power structure." [75]

Marx's theory approves such an analysis in a general way; however, democratic centralism in China is merely a strongly deformed version of a temporary state system necessary when workers, the class with profound, economic force (alongside, eventually, other classes like peasants, under certain historical circumstances), democratically elect deputies for the purpose of self-determination.

3.7. The Connection between Democracy, Economy and Class Struggle

The CCP is very well aware of the dangers, brought about by the interests of the national bourgeoisie, of equating the development of democracy with the development of capitalism in China. This model would bring about a model according to Western democracy. So it would be wrong "to believe that the development of the market economy can naturally bring about

---

[75] "权力结构，是代表民意的立法权高于行政权和司法权，形成民主集中制，我国的人民代表大会制度就是这种权力结构。" (ibid.)

the continuous rise of the mentality and the capability of citizens participating in politics and then bring the development of democratic politics naturally." [76]

The national, economic foundation has tended to shift in favor of capitalism since the period of "Reform and Opening", namely in favor of the national and international bourgeoisie, brought about by intensified privatization of state enterprises in the 1990s and the admission of the People's Republic to the World Trade Organization at the end of 2001, to only name some key events. The increasing influence of capital on the national economy pushes the development of productive forces and the numbers of workers, which is a basic factor for the development of workers creating their own world both within the materialistic sphere and in politics. The downside is the growth of inequality, correlates with economic development in the direction of capitalism.

Concerning the property structure of the means of production, the economy is still based on the basic system of socialist

---

[76] "二是认为市场经济的发展自然会带来公民政治参与意识和能力的不断提高，也就自然会带来民主政治的发 展。" （大力加强公民意识教育 公民意识教育有利于民主政治发展, 张志明, 2009.06.10)

economy, it's not a democracy of a minority, it's a democracy of the most numerous people. [77] China's democracy is directly linked with, but not just determined by the economic basis, which is why the control of capital is essential for a socialist economy. On the one side, the party has a strong influence on the economic structure as a decisive factor for the state, on the other side, the mechanisms of capitalism have extended their influence in China, which can very well be observed by the historical development of the "Reform and Opening" policy: First capitalism was a phenomenon only tolerated in a few coastal cities, while now, capitalist mechanisms are introduced all over China. Since the break out of the world financial crisis, the effects of the recession of the world market could clearly be seen in the coastal areas, which are especially dependent on export sectors. China cannot isolate itself from the tendencies of international capital, and must also handle the negative consequences of capital, including the growth of equality and the vulnerability to crisis.

In the private sector, the national and the international bourgeoisie, and the bureaucracy in the state sector,

---

[77] "这就从经济基础上决定了中国的民主不受资本的操纵，不是少数人的民主，是最广大人民的民主。" (独具特色的政治发展道路——如何理解"中国式民主" 2009.08.31.)

respectively control the means of production, whereby the overwhelming part of the working class sees itself outside the decision-making process of the production structure.

The controversial role the CCP finds itself playing, as a deputy for the people instead of being a deputy directly of the people, can be seen in another example. The CCP verbally represents a pro-democracy position by repeating and ensuring that the party grants democracy.

So it's made clear to us repeatedly, that "'Democracy with Chinese characteristics' is a democracy with democratic centralism as an essential organizational principle and a way of activity." [78] The given system of democracy in the state structure can, for the reasons given, only be seen as a pole of attraction for the masses of the people to engage in decision-making processes to a very limited extend. However, out of its institutional development, it carries the potential for a broad forum, as the basis for a real democratic structure of the people. The precondition is the necessity to break open the old state structures and make them accessible to the people, making them an instrument controlled by the people. Given the real power structures and mechanisms used by the CP, this option seems highly unlikely under given conditions, although

---

[78] "它是以民主集中制为根本组织原则和活动方式的民主。" (ibid.)

not entirely excluded in a situation where the working class, together with others, gains dominance within the institutions given.

Although on a theoretical level the topic of class struggle takes a central place in the concept of Karl Marx as well as in the one of Mao Zedong, the question of violence is barely discussed in the context of democracy. In one text, the party strongly opposes anarchist conduction of class struggle by using mass movements. [79]

What we can observe by this statement is the rejection of any direct, emancipated way to go in the direction of emancipation of the people. Mass incidents are increasing in recent years. The working class are more and more often aware of their own, decisive factor in history; the working class finds a way in mass activities to express demands which mostly do not exceed legislation, but demand compliance with legislation, for example, the payment of the minimum wage, compensation for accidents at work, payment of retirement money etc. These are moments of self-organization and a way for workers to express their will publicly in a collective way. This form of self-

---

[79] "反对无政府主义的"大民主" (独具特色的政治发展道路——如何理解"中国式民主" 2009.08.31.)

empowerment threatens the power of local bureaucrats on the one hand and is a potential danger to the stability of the state and the power of the party as such, namely if several mass actions occur synchronously and in a coordinated way. The CP, like every government in the world, is committed to maintaining social and political stability in the process of promoting the construction of democracy. Stability has the highest priority in every political or economic reform. According to the CCP, the construction of democratic politics is a gradual process, taking place "in an evolutionary way by top-down reforms."[80]

The party asserts that, "China is a socialist country, a people's democratic dictatorship which is led by the working class and based on the alliance of workers and peasants" [81].

The CCP defines itself as the vanguard of the workers, on the class basis of workers and peasants, however, that class basis is only an interpretation and description on an idealist basis, without any real control from the bottom of the members, the basis, over the top. Without this democratic control

---

[80] Liu Jianfei: Democracy and China, New World Press 2011, Beijing, p. 8
[81] "我国是工人阶级领导的、以工农联盟为基础的人民民主专政的社会主义国家。"(李江源: 最符合我国国情的民主政治制度; 江西省邓小平理论和"三个代表"重要思想研究中心教授; 2009.02.02.)

mechanism, the party constructs an independent realm of an independently operating bureaucracy with only loose links to the classes it seeks to represent - it follows its own purpose.

Occasionally, we can find some more detailed concepts of what such democratic processes could look like, in the form of a top-down concept, as well as bottom-up concept.

One article listed four certain kinds of democratic decision making for politicians, supporting a top-down concept of democracy, including:

(1) Research about people's will

(2) Public announcements

(3) Public hearings

(4) Consultation of experts for proof of a project.

Generally, these are all important parts of a democratic structure and show a slow approach towards a more democratic society by improving people's participation and intervention in the political process and the 'scientific nature', the control by the people to a limited degree. However, the approach is a reformist one, showing that the party does not consider the people as being capable of representing themselves and their own, common interests, and rather show a consultative character with the purpose of improving the capability of the CCP to govern the people, which again promotes stability of society.[82]

Also, terms like "people's will" are always discussed in a way which does not suit the theoretical approach of Marx, as they have the character of an instruction for party members, deputies with the duty of the administration of society. This does not fit the philosophy of materialist thinking, where humanity's reality develops out of the practice of human life.

Following the suggested approach of the coaching of party members in order to improve bottom-up structures in decision-making, certain skills are needed. As mentioned above, even Hu Jintao refers to the same tradition of ancient Greek democracy as Marx did. "Democracy is not only an idea, it rather is a skill, it consists of a series of concrete links. This is why citizens not only need democratic passion, but also need to learn democratic skills accordingly."[83] The article further mentions concrete technical skills the people have to handle,

---

[82]　民主决策的若干形式　邹少欢，2011.03.16.

[83]　"民主不仅是一种理念，更是一种技术，是由一系列具体环节构成的。因此，城市居民不但要有民主的热情，还要学习有关民主的技术。"（居民自治是民主的学校（观点），2011.01.12.）

which need to be formed and completed in order to develop some kind of electoral democracy with Chinese characteristics; for example, voter registration, nomination of candidates, the voting procedure etc.

> "However, we have to be aware that the education about awareness of civic obligations we face in China is relatively lagging, especially the citizens' idea of the socialist-democratic rule of law, freedom and equality, fairness and justice, all need to be urgently strengthened. On the side of the development of the socialist democratic politics, we should prevent (...) that nowadays people's awareness of civic obligations is too small, the ability to participate in political affairs is still too low and one cannot be impatient to develop socialist democratic politics. In fact (...) we must follow the development of economic society." [84]

Accordingly, the capability of the people to rule themselves is brought into question.

Democracy requires education and skill, but in the Chinese

---

[84] "但必须看到，当前我国的公民意识教育还比较滞后，尤其是公民的社会主义民主法治、自由平等、公平正义理念亟待加强。在发展社会主义民主政治方面，应注意(...)人民群众的公民意识淡薄，政治参与能力还比较低，不能急于发展社会主义民主政治。事实上(...)必须随着经济社会的发展而不断深化。"　(大力加强公民意识教育　公民意识教育有利于民主政治发展, 张志明, 2009.06.10.)

debate, it is a skill which, metaphorically speaking, the master teaches to his student. According to materialist philosophy of Marx, the students, or humanity in general, must have all economic, educational and social requirements to abolish the master-student relation.

Having an elite concept, where the master is driven by a different motivation to the student, the interests of the rulers and the people do not equate - the CCP does not have an interest in abolishing their own role as a masters.

Even though the ability to rule themselves is not given to the people, or only to a small extent, by the CP, the latter creates the material conditions for worker's democracy. The ongoing transformation of peasants to workers, expressed by a mass migration and urbanization, is taken place in an extremely fast time, historically considered. In a nation where the peasants traditionally predominated the urban population, the percentage of the rural population fell to 50.5% in 2010, while the number of migrant workers, people who decide to leave the countryside to become a wage earner, often in factories, increased rapidly. This economic transformation pushes the productive forces and creates the relevant preconditions for worker's democracy, the productive part of the population with the capability of creating material welfare as well as democratic conditions for the people.

One important precondition for the participation of people in a democratic process is the willingness of the people to participate, which is closely linked to people's consciousness as a species. Once human consciousness is collectively aware of its creative potential, it can suggest a collective, socialist way of society and can decide on questions about procedure and organization of society, for example in which way elections can be useful for people's interests. Unless the concept suggestion of the CCP, the development of society in general and democracy in this specific case, is not a gradual, but a dialectic process, happening irregularly in leaps.

The question of ownership and power of disposal, which is closely linked to the question of democracy, must not be brought about by the bureaucracy, but must be brought forward by the workers as a question of emancipation of the people. This is how Marx deals with this question in his writings.

3.8. Democratic Potentials

It is obvious that, in a nation as big as China, there will be 'democratic contraction' on a regular basis. According to the CP's ideology formulated in the newspaper researched on, there are conflicts between different layers of the population. For example, pupils and parents who want a gym for their school or people in certain areas who ask for democratic elections. All projects need a certain amount of focus and resources of the government, the government has to balance these resources and cannot satisfy all groups equally, especially if the interests are contradictory: For instance, a factory owner wants lower environment regulations, the villagers protest for more (this example is not directly given in the People's Daily). The CCP is forced to ask the question how to solve these contradictions in an appropriate way, so that harm for society and more importantly the leadership is limited. Here, the task is to find innovative, "new democratic participation channels."[85]

So the CP's problem scenario concerning democratic contradictions.

---

[85] "建设新的民主参与渠道 "   (建设新的民主参与渠道; 周天鸿 2010.03.12.)

Especially in rural problem areas, where conventional methods of strictly top-down mechanisms do not work anymore, the introduction of democratic mechanisms is seen as an alternative. "In some villages, where the contradiction is prominent, it is by relying on expanding democracy to take care of public utilities, straighten out the mood of the masses and achieve harmony and stability" [86] by leading top-down and bottom-up mechanisms together.

Beside the possibilities already discussed, for example law, democratic management etc., the party is very well aware of the favorable, democratic potential of the internet and the CCP already uses it for communication and the educational advertising of inner party decisions, which effect the whole of society (top-down policy), but avoids using it for the active participation of the broad masses of the people in the decision-making processes (bottom-up policy). "Internet forums, online voting, online surveys, short messages etc., this 'internet participation' is fast and comfortable and contributes enormously to rise the quality of democratic participation."[87]

---

[86] "在一些矛盾比较突出的重点村庄，正是依靠扩大民主的办法，办好了公共事业，理顺了群众情绪，实现了和谐稳定。" (民主之花 精彩绽放（两会感言），李章军, 2010.03.06.)

[87] "网上论坛、网上投票、网上调查、手机短信等"在线参与"快捷方便，大大提高了民主参与的效率。" (发挥网络文化在发展民主

The bureaucracy, without any actual class controlling their action and with only a rhetorical commitment to the working class, is mainly obligated to its inner party group dynamics, its own bureaucratic interest. The only way workers can influence the bureaucracy is by class struggle, i.e. threatening the power of the CCP with demonstrating its economic force, which reminds them of their self-imposed commitment about who the party ultimately represents. Such an act of emancipation, which only finds short notice in the debate, can push the leadership to act in favor of a working class which are at the same time a threat to stability and the CCP's rule, if those class struggles take place outside the party and officially legitimated structures.

We can see that the CCP is representing the people in a way that serves their own interests first and that they have close links to the national bourgeoisie. Besides this, we can see a strong commitment and a claim to be really building true democracy. Even though small in number, there are very progressive contributions in articles, defining the goal of democracy as to make people "masters of their own affairs" and "freedom":

政治中的作用, 宋元林, 2009.04.08.)

"'Democracy' as the search for a real value, a core value system of socialism, establishes a more perfect essence of socialist democratic politics, lets people enjoy the right to be masters of their own affairs and more freedom, and creates good politic conditions for 'people's freedom and universal development'."[88]

We can see references to Marx and Engels in a philosophical context, associated with the topic of democracy:

"Marx and Engels clearly proclaim in the 'Communist Manifesto': "In place of the old bourgeois society, with its classes and class antagonisms, we shall have an association, in which the free development of each is the condition for the free development of all""[89] [90]

---

88 "民主"作为社会主义核心价值体系的现实价值追求，其实质是建立更为完善的社会主义民主政治，让人民群众享有当家作主的权利和更充分的自由，为"人的自由而全面的发展"创造良好的政治条件"; (富强、民主、文明、和谐; 社会主义核心价值体系的基本价值理念，龙兴海，杨高岚，2009.08.28.)

89 "马克思和恩格斯在《共产党宣言》中明确宣示: "代替那存在着阶级和阶级对立的资产阶级旧社会的，将是这样一个联合体，在那里，每个人的自由发展是一切人的自由发展的条件。" 马克思在《资本论》中也明确指出，共产主义是"以每个人的全面而自由的发展为基本原则的社会形式。"随着时代的发展，科学社会主义理论也在不断发展和完善，但以"人的自由而全面的发展"为基本原则和根本追求一直是科学社会主义坚持的基本原理和宗旨。因此，实现"人的自由而全面的发展"，是中国特色社会主义的本质要求，也是社会主义核心价值体系的基本价值理念。" (ibid.)

90 Marx, Karl: Manifesto of the Communist Party, Chapter II: Proletarians

We can clearly see the ideas that also inspired Mao in his writings and the young communists movement in practice in Yan'an, which later on became a model for the whole of China. The same quotation states that Marx also clearly announced in 'Capital' that communism is "the real basis of a higher form of society, a society in which the full and free development of every individual forms the ruling principle."[91]

Obviously, China is still far away from reaching preconditions under which individuals can develop freely, first of all economic ones. Compared to the industrial countries there is still a big gap China has to catch up, considering GDP figures. One of the historic achievements of Marx was that he could explain the tendencies of capitalism at an early stage – such as the accumulation of capital and its vulnerability to crisis - in a scientific way by analyzing contemporary economic theories and figures available. This tendency to crisis is nowadays more actual than ever: Through the fall of the Soviet Union and it's global consequences, the capitalist system is more dominant on

---

and Communists, 1848.

[91] Marx, Karl: Capital Volume 1, Chapter 42: Conversion of Surplus-Value into Capital, Section 3 - Separation of Surplus-Value into Capital and Revenue - The Abstinence Theory.
online source: www.marxists.org/archive/marx/works/1867-c1/ch24.htm seen 01.03.214

a world scale than ever, so global consequences of the crises appear in every country connected to global economy. Now, the CP, referring to Marx and scientific socialism, states in the same article mentioned above that in the course of time Marx's theory of scientific socialism is also continuously developing and completing. But according to Marxist philosophy 'the full and free development of every individual' as the real principle and basic goal is Marx' scientific socialism's persisting fundamental principle and aim. Therefore, the realization of 'the full and free development of every individual' is the basic demand of the 'socialism with Chinese characteristics', and the basic value of the core value system of socialism. This statement of the People's Daily authors is identical with Marx' theory, although Marxist theory focuses on the liberation of the individual in a collective way.

In this last argument we can see proof that the CCP does not refer directly to the methodology of Marx but considers it as changing with time. The decisions of different Chinese leaders, from Mao Zedong to Deng Xiaoping, Jiang Zemin and Hu Jintao were logical developments of the philosophical foundation, including political program, method and tradition. For example, the change in program by Deng Xiaoping puts

Chinese state ideology in the light of necessity to an opening up to capitalism, although the official argument also does not put the revolution and the construction of a 'new China' by Mao in question. This change in state ideology is described as a logical transformation of Marx's theory. It does not take into account that different factions inside the CCP stand for different ways of policy-making.

Naturally, the world did change after Marx finished the manuscripts on 'Capital' and passed away, however, the fundamental mechanisms of the system of capitalism stayed the same: In the Western world, they expanded enormously, relatively to the 19th century, and China also consequently accepted the introduction of foreign capital and the laws of capitalism, even though they are partly under the control of the bureaucracy.

In the discourse about democracy, the CCP delineates itself from the Western model with the argument that Western democratic theorists see the democracy model developed in Europe as the only legitimate one, including criteria like Western-style elections and multi-party competition. The CCP instead considers itself as a vanguard party according to the

Leninist tradition, ruling on behalf of the working class as the dictatorship of the proletariat.

Furthermore, democracy is discussed in the context of Hu Jintao's concept of harmony. Class interests and consequently class struggles find no theoretical expression in its theoretical and practical discourse. Though, according to the theory of Marx, as we can see in practice, the ruling bureaucracy has to make concessions to the working class. Therefore, the CCP's theory meets Marx's category of a Hegelian (idealistic) understanding of society, ignoring the working class as an active part in creating history and deciding on their own mode of democracy.

4. Democracy and Marx

4.1. The young Marx

This chapter will deal with Marx's own philosophy concerning the idea of democracy. In every great philosopher's life, the thinker's ideas develop and change by improvement and experience from his early years to his later works, although the general arguments often remain the same. This is also the case with Karl Marx's philosophical ideas, from his youth to his later years. In his early years, Marx adapted the transcendental ideas of Hegel, which made him a radical democrat and inspired his overall work. Even though Hegel was an idealist thinker, Marx showed a deep interest in the Young Hegelians, essentially because of the group's critical views on religion.

According to Avineri, one theory in literature is that around 1843, in his early years, when the 25 year old Marx wrote the 'Critique of Hegel's Philosophy of Right', Marx's political solution was merely democratic - the overall concept of communism only appeared later in his writings. Marx's democracy, which he also calls "true democracy", is not fundamentally different from his later concept of "communism". "True democracy" is the state of society where there is no alienation between man and the political structure, a process introduced by the later described dissolution of state. At this time, he developed an idea of society based on the abolition of private property and the dissolution of the state. With the atomization of civil society (bürgerliche Gesellschaft), the common wealth (Gemeinwesen) and the "communist essence" (das kommunistische Wesen) are divorced from the state - the political state nowadays is an abstraction of that state.[92]

In the same writing Marx argues that "democracy in the constitution, the law, the state, so far as it is political constitution, is itself only a self-determination *of* the people, and a determinate content *of* the people." [emphasis by the author][93]

---

[92] Avineri, Shromo: The Social and Political Thought of Karl Marx,. Cambridge University Press 1968, London, chapter "True Democracy" p. 31-41
[93] Ibid.

4.2. The later Marx

Marx discovered, in his search for a path to true democracy, that there were contradictions within the system that would not allow the emancipation of humanity as a whole, the overcoming of the atomization of civil society, the common wealth and the communist essence. These contradictions are class contradictions, i.e. two opposing classes standing in contrast to each other. At this point it was therefore clear that in order to overcome class contradictions, the overcoming of the capitalist system is crucial. Real democracy is therefore only possible if the system changes.

Marx and Engels often referred to the utopian socialists of their time and sharpened their position and strategy by criticizing them, i.e. criticizing ideologies which seek to change the world by mere ideas, ignoring conditions given by the material world.

4.3. Marx about Democracy

Karl Marx himself also wrote about democracy that modern states call themselves democratic, but fail to be so.[94]

---

[94] Marx, Karl: Critique of Hegel's Philosophy of Right, 1843; chapter 1,

Democracy is about class rule, and true democracy is the rule of the majority, especially the working class. "[T]he first step in the revolution by the working class, is to raise the proletariat to the position of ruling class, to win the battle of democracy." [95] It is closely connected, if not identical with scientific socialism, i.e. Marx's conception of communism.

The topic of democracy was never his main focus; democracy is a topic co-opted by the petty bourgeoisie, and therefore has a problematic connotation in the purpose of human emancipation because the debate is often misleading, as I will argue later. The numbers are taken from the categorization, found in the German subject index to Marx Engels Werke.[96] The edition of Marx and Engels, produced in 39 volumes, plus a two-part supplementary volume produced in Berlin by the Dietz publisher 1968, constitutes the basis for the "Sachregister" (subject index). Those sub-categories of the key word

---

The Constitution
online source: www.marxists.org/archive/marx/works/1843/critique-hpr/ch02.htm seen on 12.11.2014

[95] Marx Engels Werke, Dietz Verlag Berlin, DDR 1968, Vol. 16, p. 5-13, 10.1864; online source: http://www.marxists.org/deutsch/archiv/marx-engels/1864/10/inaugadr.htm seen 02.02.2015

[96] Dr. Willi Herferth (Institut für Geschichte der deutschen Arbeiterbewegung der Akademie für Geschichtswissenschaften b. ZK der SED): Sachregister zu den Werken (edition 1–39+2). Pahl-Rugenstein Verlag GmbH, Köln 1983; keyword: Demokratie (p. 171-175)

"Democracy" are listed in the table below and are to be found in the "Sachregister" on pages 171-175. Of course, the index is not computer generated and therefore reflects the interests of the persons it has been compiled by, including the author Willi Herferth.The connotation is chosen according to examples from the sub-categories. According to Marx's writing style it can be easily concluded whether, in Marx's view, he considers a certain discourse (sub-category) positive or negative for the overall goals of the working class; for example, petty bourgeois democracy, the majority category in the set of articles about democracy, has a clearly negative connotation, as I will argue later. Let's have a look at a listing of passages, where Marx relates to democracy, and see if he refers to it with an overwhelmingly positive or negative attitude.

Democracy as...	nr. of passages
- petty bourgeois democracy, weaknesses and reactionary tendencies	566
- bourgeois democracy, mendacity	66
- alliance between the proletariat and the petty bourgeoisie	34
- bourgeois democracy, expression of disguise of class contradiction between bourgeoisie and working class	17
- defeat of democracy in Germany	6
~ democracy and national liberty	5
~ it's conception by the working class and it's role for the development of the working class	119
~ support by the working class	50
~ democracy and social revolution, context	40
~ in ancient times	7
~ petty bourgeois democracy as a form of class struggle between proletariat and petty bourgeois parties	7
+ it's full unfolding as precondition for a socialist revolution (especially for petty bourgeois democracy)	36
+ as transition stage to real liberty	25
+ as a means to defend worker's rights and enforcement of its demands against private property	24
mainly negative connotation	689
mainly neutral connotation	228
mainly positive connotation	85
total	1002

Key: - sign: negative connotation; ~ sign: neutrale connotation;+ sign: negative connotation

We can see that in more than a third of the articles where Marx mentions democracy, democracy plays a negative role, and only 8.5% relate positively to the term of democracy. We can conclude that the predominant interpretation of democracy is a problematic one in Marxist philosophy. The example of the Chinese debate about democracy and its comparison with Marx's philosophy, including discussions about real democracy, state power, the emancipation of the workers etc., will support this argument.

4.4. Formally introduced Democracy: Top-Down

Marx's main criticism of Hegel indicated that the latter did not promote "real democracy", but instead democracy as a superficial change which would not change the basic contradictions, namely that "the democratic element can be admitted only as a formal element in a state organism that is merely a formalism of the state. The democratic element should be, rather, the actual element that acquires its rational form in the whole organism of the state. If the democratic element enters the state organism or state formalism as a particular element, then the rational form of its existence means a drill, an accommodation, a form, in which it does not exhibit what is characteristic of its essence. In other words, it would enter the state organism merely as a formal principle."[97]

Real democracy is a powerful tool and with its establishment systematic changes can come about. On the other hand, democracy as a formality can be easily established, but does not initialize an emancipatory process. The essence of democracy therefore is a general effect on society, not a particular one.

4.5. Democracy as a Means for Socialism

Instead of the promotion of democracy, which is only there to improve the mechanisms for the rule of a minority and the rich, the capitalists or big bourgeoisie, Engels promotes the fight of the poor against the rich as a fight for democracy, which pushes in a socialist direction. In this way, democracy is a vehicle for socialism and democracy can be interpreted as a tactical tool for a social democracy, which is a transmission - the last, political means which people use to achieve economic equality. Because real democracy inside the governmental system is

---

[97] Marx, Karl: Critique of Hegel's Philosophy of Right, written 1843, Oxford University Press, 1970; online source: http://www.marxists.org/archive/marx/works/1843/critique-hpr/ch06.htm seen 20.03.2014

limited, formalized and institutionalized, another element will grow out of this struggle, a principle develops, which exceeds the political being: This is the principle of socialism.[98]

Marx and Engels both connect the struggle for a general democratization to the systematic question.

Engels further argues that democracy is, in all forms of government, an inherent contradiction, a hypocrisy. Political freedom is illusory freedom, the worst kind of slavery, pseudo-freedom and therefore the worst kind of subjugation.[99]

For example, the social reform movement in France in the first half of the 19th century came to the conclusion that democracy as a formal tool is not a vehicle to reach real equality, which is why the system of communes was to be used.[100] As a key contribution to the topic of direct democracy, Marx and Engels analyzed a contemporary historical example for 'real democracy': The Paris Commune (1871) was under worker's control from February 23rd 1848 to December 2nd 1848. On

---

[98] Marx Engels Gesamtausgabe, Dietz Verlag Berlin DDR, Vol. 1, 1975, p.592
[99] Marx Engels Gesamtausgabe, Dietz Verlag Berlin, DDR, Vol. 1, 1975, p.481
[100] Ibid.

December 10th the nephew of the former French emperor Lois Napoléon Bonaparte was elected president.

4.6. Class analysis and Class Contradictions

In Marxist philosophy there are basic class contradictions between the two opposing classes. What are those classes?

Engels defines the proletariat as "that class in society which lives entirely from the sale of its labor and does not draw profit from any kind of capital; whose weal and woe, whose life and death, whose sole existence depends on the demand for labor".[101]

Workers sell their labor and a part of the surplus value of this labor is taken by the capitalist or bourgeois, a French word meaning 'the trading middle class'. This minority owns the means of production, including factories, machines etc. Those who work, the producers, only own and sell their labor. In this system, those who create value get the smallest share of the wealth, which is just enough to cover their reproduction

---

[101] Marx and Engels: Selected Works, Volume One, p. 81-97, Progress Publishers, 1969 Moscow, article first published: 1914 by Eduard Bernstein in the German Social Democratic Party's newspaper "*Vorwärts!*"

expenses, as Marx calls it, i.e. to cover life expenses for food and rent, to raise children etc., while the bourgeoisie is "the class of modern capitalists, owners of the means of social production and employers of wage labor".[102]

The main problem is not that the bourgeoisie waste their profits, but that these few people decide what to produce and where the surplus is invested. The overage is not necessarily invested in goods - only the capitalist can decide if, for instance, vacuum cleaners or machine guns are produced.

The capitalist cannot exploit the workers, who outnumber him, all on his own. He builds a whole apparatus around him to make the exploitation work politically, comparable with a military command structure:

> "An industrial army of workmen, under the command of a capitalist, requires, like a real army, officers (managers) and sergeants (foremen, overlookers) who, while the work is being done, command in the name of the capitalist".[103]

This is the origin of hierarchy in the production process. The mechanism described is necessary for the capitalist to maintain his production regime, guaranteeing him profit without

---

[102] Marx and Engels: 'Manifesto of the Communist Party' in: Karl Marx: 'Selected Works', Vol. 1; London; 1943; p. 204
[103] Marx, Karl: Capital: An Analysis of Capitalist Production, Moscow; 1959, Volume 1, p. 332

contributing to the production, but controlling it. On the one hand he takes a disproportionate share of the working class's produced surplus value, on the other hand he controls the productive forces; this is how the working class gives up its sovereignty, by subordination to the needs of the minority of capitalists. While the capitalist is in control of the production process and benefits economically from his commanding position, the working class is alienated form its daily creative work, it is under control of a minority with a shared interest in contrast to those of the working class. This phenomenon is not only limited to the economic basis, but affects the whole of society.

After revealing the basic class analysis of society, let's have a look at the criteria of what Marx and Engels consider petty bourgeois requests or real democratic requests in the daily, political struggle.

The International Workers Association (IWA), better known as the 'First International' was founded by workers inspired by Marx, following his slogan "Workers of all countries, unite!" in the spirit of internationalism. The organization condemned "la démocratie vulgaire" (vulgar democracy), the idea of formally providing political rights to workers in order to leave the privileges of the middle and upper class untouched. The IWA had gone through experiences with the Italian and French democratic bourgeoisie, that wanted to use the International for these purposes[104].

Once coming to power and therefore under the influence of the ruling class, the class character of this so-called democratic bourgeoisie, those promoters of "la démocratie vulgaire", is obvious. They follow their own class basis, which is petty bourgeois, instead of representing proletarian interests in general or real workers' democracy in particular.

Engels criticized the petty bourgeoisie's request for pure democratic demands and opposed the legislation by the people, giving the example of Switzerland, where, already during his lifetime, the negative effects of petty bourgeois democracy overweight the positive. Instead, he requires the administration *of* the people, namely direct administration.

---

[104] Engels to Carlo Cafiero in Nepal, London, 28.07.1871. Marx Engels Werke, Dietz Verlag Berlin, 1975, Vol. 33, p. 664

4.7. Idealism and Materialism: Marx and Bakunin

Marx identified petty bourgeois, reactionary tendencies as one problem of the 'Internationale' which had some influence within the organization and provoked confusion. Bakunin had been an executive committee of "Ligue de la Paix et de la Liberté" (League of Peace and Freedom), a petty bourgeois organization, before joining the IWA, opposed Marx's ideas and caused central conflicts:

Bakunin's former organization supported the goals of peace and freedom. It sought to abolish the army and supported several democratic requests, without any class analysis to base these demands on. That's why Marx considered its program as illusory.

Marx opposed the sectarian character of Bakunin's intension to take over the association and his petty bourgeois theoretical approach; Marx summarized the latter as follows:

(1) Abolition of hereditary right.

(2) Equality of class differences, merely by definition.

(3) Not allowing the working class to become involved in politics, though it may organize in trade unions.

This program consists of wishes, which want society to ideologically improve, but are not linked to society materialistically. It was not developed out of practice, therefore theory and practice are not linked: it is pure metaphysics.[105]

Marx, on the other hand, represented an independent, proletarian class character of the IWA. In such a way, the everyday reality of workers' experience directly found its path to policy.

Historically, Marx and Engels made the experience that the democratic parties of the moderate bourgeoisie in Germany were happy to make compromises with the ruling class. On one side, they show a progressive character against absolutism; on the other, they will make compromises with the ruling class and support it. This is how those moderate bourgeois parties turn against true democracy. Marx also speaks out against doubts: "We must clearly warn against those hypocritical friends who, while declaring that they agree with the principles, doubt whether they are practicable, because, they allege, the world is not yet ready for them, and who have no

---

[105] Marx to Paul and Laura Laforrgue in Paris. London, 19.04.1840. in Marx Engels Werke (German edition), Vol. 32, p. 673-678

intention of making it ready, but on the contrary prefer to share the common lot of the wicked in this wicked earthly life."[106]

4.8. Class Interest: Economic basis and Superstructure

"Political, juridical, philosophical, religious, literary, artistic, etc. development is based on economic development. But these all react on one another and also upon the economic basis. It is not that the economic situation is cause, solely active, while everything else is only passive effect. There is rather interaction on the basis of economic necessity which ultimately always asserts itself."[107]

The objective conditions applied in the production process make up a big part of workers' lives and influence this historical subject. This is where the superstructure comes into play: The capitalists' control reaches out beyond the production process, deep into society. By the daily control of workers'

---

[106] Marx and Engels: "Neue Rheinische Zeitung", Nr. 2, 2.6.1848, online source:
http://www.marxists.org/archive/marx/works/download/Marx_Articles_from_the_NRZ.pdf, p.23, seen 20.06.2014

[107] Engels to W. Borgius, Letter of 25 January 1894. in Marx Engels Werke 1968 (German Edition), Berlin, Vol. 39, p. 206; English online source:
http://www.marxists.org/archive/marx/works/1894/letters/94_01_25.htm seen 15.01.2015

lives through the production process, mechanisms of dominance and control, originating form the economic basis, extend to the superstructure, i.e. policy making, jurisdiction, legislation, art and, of course, democracy - namely, the whole of society. In an inversion of the argument, the basis of all societal improvements lies in the economy. According to this insight, true democracy can only be established in a process of a general change of the economic basis, followed by a general change of the superstructure.

As Marx described in the process of the French revolution, which led to the construction of the Paris Commune 1871, the main principles of the state mechanisms were changed: The standing army was replaced by general military service of an extremely short period of time, so that the people exercised executive power as directly as possible by themselves. The "educational institutions were opened to the people gratuitously, and at the same time cleared of all interference of church and state" and the judicial functionaries of the old regime

> "were to be divested of that sham independence which had but served to mask their abject subserviency_to all succeeding governments to which, in turn, they had taken, and broken, the

> oaths of allegiance. Like the rest of public servants, magistrates and judges were to be elective, responsible, and revocable."[108]

We can see that the mechanisms of the social system were changed. A system with the purpose of keeping a privileged majority in power was, by all kind of institutional turns, changed into a system to serve society, the community - the commune. By those changes in a very short period of time, the individual was not yet completely emancipated, however a common direction with the ultimate goal of emancipation was given and the commune made a first step towards this purpose. This decision can be described as truly democratic, because its purpose is the freedom of the empowered individual within the commune.

4.9. Class Contradictions

In capitalism, during its creative production, the worker loses the part of the surplus value he created. The struggle over the surplus value causes a permanent struggle about power and influence on the political level. The capitalists will influence

---

[108] Marx, Karl: The Civil War in France; May, 1871, chapter The Paris Commune,
online source: www.marxists.org/archive/marx/works/1871/civil-war-france/ch05.htm, seen 07.2013

the policy system by every means possible to fulfill their purpose of the private disposition of that surplus value.

Hence, the economic struggle for the common fruits of production among the workers and the owner of the means of production is immanent in the capitalist system. Thereby, the capitalist's interest is to limit economic and political rights, for the capitalist directly has to hand over those profits he grants the worker. The interest of the working class is the opposite of the interest of the capitalist, namely the distribution of the fruits of labor: The working class wants to reinvest it for the direct purpose of society, while the capitalist class wants to use it for its own private purpose.

Furthermore, the capitalists use capacities to influence the state, i.e. policy-making systems like those institutions described before – the education system, the police and army: jurisdictions to improve their mechanism of control with the purpose of using them for their own interest and driving them in their direction. Thereby the state, as an original representational organ of society, changes into an institution for the exploitation, control and alienation of society under capitalism.

One important indicator in the level of alienation between

representatives and the people might be the level of corruption inside the state apparatus, meaning that the bureaucracy are not democratically controlled by society, but follow their own private, material interests. So, in this quote Marx argues for the self-governance of the people against the corrupt, capitalist government of former France, when he comments on the Commune de Paris:

> "Peculiar historical circumstances may have prevented the classical development, as in France, of the bourgeois form of government, and may have allowed, as in England, to complete the great central state organs by corrupt vestries, jobbing councilors, and ferocious poor-law guardians in the towns, and virtually hereditary magistrates in the counties.

> The Communal Constitution would have restored to the social body all the forces hitherto absorbed by the state parasite feeding upon, and clogging the free movement of society. By this one act, it would have initiated the regeneration of France."[109]

Marx focuses on the communal constitution, which was worked out from direct and real representatives in a very democratic, grassroots discussion, a forum of all the people, including women and workers, i.e. the direct representatives of

---

[109] Marx, Karl: The Civil War in France; The Third Address; May, 1871, Chapter The Paris Commune,
online source: www.marxists.org/archive/marx/works/1871/civil-war-france/ch05.htm

mass population, sharing their material fate and their interests and fighting side by side for true democracy in Paris.

4.10. The Transformation to Socialism

A transformation to socialism means to change those mechanisms inherent in the capitalist system that lead to the exploitation of man. This process takes time to develop. A wish does not take material forms just because the wish is articulated, but there needs to be a democratic decision by the majority for such a change, based on the reality of man. In such a momentum, the determined takes the place of the determining, the predicate turns into the subject. A revolution takes place and the working class establishes itself as the determining subject.

Assuming that the working class is controlled by the capitalist class, with the help of the bureaucracy, detached from the working class, a shift of power, i.e. a revolution, is necessary to change the influence of the capitalists and the bureaucracy and bring the working class into power. This is how 'atomization' of society is overcome and 'true democracy' brought about. In this process, man changes from a suppressed subject, a mere predicate, to a subject, a free person; finally man and his social activity become one and the same thing: emancipated society means emancipated self, which Marx calls "man's communist essence" (das kommunistische Wesen des Menschen) or "socialized man" (der sozialisierte Mensch).[110]

4.11. The Question of Representation

Regarding the question of representation, the working class faces a dilemma. Can it gain control through representatives? Are they necessary, or harmful because they endanger the path to freedom?

The approach of Marx regarding the question of the Paris Commune 1871 can give us further insight: In a historic situation, the workers of the city took over all of the state structure and governing instruments of the old state, and turned them into instruments of self-governance of the collective:

> "The Commune [was] to consist of the municipal councilors of the different *arrondissements* (as Paris was the initiator and the model, we have to refer to it), chosen by the suffrage of all citizens, responsible,

---

[110] Avineri, Shromo: The Social and Political Thought of Karl Marx, Cambridge University Press 1968, London; chapter "True Democracy" p. 31-41

and revocable in short terms. The majority of that body would naturally consist of workmen or acknowledged representatives of the working class. It was to be a working, not a parliamentary body, executive and legislative at the same time. The police agents, instead of being the agents of a central government, were to be the servants of the Commune, having, like the functionaries in all the other departments of administration, to be appointed and always revocable by the Commune; all the functionaries, like the members of the Commune itself, having to do their work at workmen's wages. The judges were also to be elected, revocable, and responsible. The initiative in all matters of social life to be reserved to the Commune. In one word, all public functions, even the few ones that would belong to the Central Government, were to be executed by Communal agents, and, therefore, under the control of the Commune. It is one of the absurdities to say that the Central functions, not of governmental authority over the people, but necessitated by the general and common wants of the country, would become impossible. These functions would exist, but the functionaries themselves could not, as in the old governmental machinery, raise themselves over real society, because the functions were to be executed by *Communal agents*, and, therefore, always under real control."[111]

So we can see a kind of representation that is new and different in essence, relative to the old one. Direct control of the working class itself and the abolishment of the executive and

---

[111] Marx, Karl: The Civil War in France; The Third Address; May, 1871, Chapter The Paris Commune,
online source: www.marxists.org/archive/marx/works/1871/civil-war-france/ch05.htm, seen 07.2013

legislative avoids alienation of the representatives and the limitation of their wage to that one of a common worker binds their material condition to that of the working class. Under capitalist conditions, functionaries follow their own interests. In the process of shift of power, representation will still be necessary over the period of time, when the people as yet cannot be emancipated by themselves. They are willing to take over power to a certain extent and move in the direction of self-emancipation gradually. In socialism, precautionary measures are taken to merge the fate of "communal agents", as Marx calls them, to those of the working class – these are true, material representatives of their class and guarantee direct democratic control of this caste of administration. So these agents must be from among the workers and share a common fate with workers.

Marx calls this most direct rule the dictatorship of the working class. By Marx's and Engels' living times, the term "dictatorship" could refer to the classical Roman institution of preservative crisis government, but the term had not yet been used for a permanent one-man rule, it only referred to a short time solution, not a continuing dictatorship it's used nowadays.

The concept of revolutionary "dictatorship" brought forward

by Marx and Engels had another meaning. "The desire to put the system of a single brain into execution by means of dictatorship deserves to be called nonsense", Marx wrote in a letter to Weitling in August 1848, "it was to be a *constituent* dictatorship (…) assumed the authority of a democratically elected constituent assembly" until the establishment of new, permanent institutions of government and a new legality. This is Marx' and Engels conception of dictatorship for a proletarian revolution.

For Marx, the mere existence of the state is an institutional expression of people's alienation, which cannot be overcome within the state itself. The social solution lies beyond the state so it will be abolished ("aufgehoben"). Man's "communist essence" is incompatible with civil society ("bürgerliche Gesellschaft") and the state.

The dictatorship of the proletariat in Marx' sense does not mean the rule on *behalf of* the people, but rule *of* the people, so the dictatorship of the few is dissolved into the rule of all, whereby bureaucracy is characterized by hierarchy and division functions.

In Engel's view, after the revolution succeeds, the state would "wither away" ("der Staat wird nicht 'abgeschafft', er stirbt ab" (Engels, also quoted by Lenin [112])), or as Marx put it, you would see the abolition and transcendence ("Aufhebung") of the state. Only if the state as a distinct, separate organization disappears can the individual achieve universal content, the state has to be dissolved in the masses, whereby the people undertake the state's former functions. In the context of proletarian rule, Marx does not use the term "dictatorship of the proletariat" and all together, he does not use it more that two or three times all together: Only in 'Critique of the Gotha Programm' and in a letter to Weydemeyer, a Marxist revolutionary and friend of Marx, on 5 March 1852[113], and indirectly in a speech on 25 September 1871.

---

[112] Engels, Friedrich: Anti-Dühring: Theoretisches (Marx Engels Werke, Vol. 20, p.261- 262), online source:
www.mlwerke.de/me/me20/me20_001.htm
also quoted by Lenin, State and Revolution, chapter1, sub-chapter 4, "Das „Absterben" des Staates und die gewaltsame Revolution", online source:
http://www.marxists.org/deutsch/archiv/lenin/1917/staatrev/kapitel1.htm#f3 seen 01.04.2014

[113] Marx: Letter to Weydemeyer on 05.03.1852. Marx Engels Werke, Vol. 28, p.503- 509

4.12. The Continuation of the old in the new Form

In a dialectical way Marx describes socialist communes, the societal micro-form for organization in socialism, as having parallels, but not to be confused with, the historic form of primitive communism and medieval communes. This new commune will have modern techniques for the means of production in their hands and will truly democratically decide over future investment, collective needs and purposes, administration and the overall production process.

> "It is generally the fate of completely new historical creations to be mistaken for the counterparts of older, and even defunct, forms of social life, to which they may bear a certain likeness. Thus, this new Commune, which breaks with the modern state power, has been mistaken for a reproduction of the medieval Communes, which first preceded, and afterward became the substratum of that very state power."[114]

Marx suggests an active process in order to decide on "communal agents": The commune can directly discuss the distribution of power among their members according to their abilities by vote and can deselect agents in case they don't do

---

[114] Marx, Karl: The Civil War in France; The Third Address; May, 1871, Chapter The Paris Commune, online source: www.marxists.org/archive/marx/works/1871/civil-war-france/ch05.htm

their duty according to the community's satisfaction. The crucial point is that real, or direct democracy must be decisive concerning the affairs the state used to be responsible for. Marx goes as far as comparing the commune with companies concerning the people's ability to decide on capable representation in the formation process towards real democracy:

> "And it is well-known that companies, like individuals, in matters of real business generally know how to put the right man in the right place, and, if they for once make a mistake, to redress it promptly. On the other hand, nothing could be more foreign to the spirit of the Commune than to supersede universal suffrage by hierarchical investiture".[115]

4.13. The Role of the Working Class

The working class is just one of many groups in society, so why does it play such an extraordinarily important role in Marxist philosophy?

The workers are the class that fulfills the task of creating objects for society. They can see a necessity and plan the creation of an object in their mind before they produce the

---

[115] Ibid.

object required with the help of tools. They actually design the materialist world of humanity on a daily basis. In the collective process of creation, i.e. the economic basis, in which man gives the world a special shape, man adopts nature according to his own needs. Workers are those human beings most capable of realizing their own role in society and shaping a different world at will.

The workers as the subject of a revolutionary change can bring about direct democracy.

With the creation of their own fate, workers will make the existence of the old state redundant. When the commune comes into being, the old state is substituted. That is a form of government where the government itself is dissolved by the people, in the people: The state is the people and the people are the state, form and content are one and the same. The barrier between individuals and collectivism fades, freedom of development is guaranteed for the individual within the framework of the collective.

At this point, the discussion about the character of the state is not necessary any more. The commune has nothing to do with the state in its original sense. In the 'Communist Manifesto' Marx states that directly after the revolution and the formation of the socialist order, the state in its original sense ceases to exist. It will dissolve in its own and disappear.

However, history has shown us that recent big scale revolutions took place in backwards countries which were isolated. The socialist order Marx mentioned could not become established in a regional, limited extent and, compared to the industrialized countries, in a state of relative backwardness. At this stage, where the old has already died but the new cannot yet be born, a new state will come into being in this stage of transformation between capitalism and socialism. This is the situation of the state in China, where the state cannot be abolished and has existed since the revolution of 1949. In this emergence of a new state, neither capitalism, nor socialism is fully established. This dilemma occurred in all backward countries where a socialist revolution took place but was not, or could not be brought to an end. In this special situation, the new state takes the role of keeping down the former ruling class with force. This is why Engels argues, "the proletariat needs the state, not in the interests of freedom but in order to hold down its adversaries, and as soon as it becomes possible to speak of freedom the state as such ceases to exist"[116].

The state as such fulfills the task of defending the commune, it is a tool of the commune for the self-defense of democratic achievements, so the legitimization of a state structure follows the purpose of a survival instinct. As soon as the danger to the commune fades away, the state will dissolve. As long as dangers exist, a state is necessary. Those countries where a socialist revolution succeeded were, most of the time, attacked or fear intervention. Consequently, the state power was, as in every national war situation, centralized and state structures were not reduced but extended - see, for example, the historical cases of the Soviet Union 1917, the People's Republic of China 1949 and Cuba in 1961 or Venezuela in 2002. The consequences for the backwards states were quite similar, the endangerment of the transforming, new state increased, resources of the already backwards state were bound for military expenses and international isolation becomes more severe due to the competition between the system of capitalism and socialism on a world wide scale. In the US, president Eisenhower put forward the domino theory in the 1950s which

---

[116] Engels to August Beel in Zwickau, London, 18./28.03.1875. Marx Engels Werke, Dietz Verlag Berlin, 1975:, Vol. 34, p. 129

explained the danger of one country after the other coming under the influence of communism, referring to communism as a danger to the US capitalist model. Furthermore, militarization like during the Cold War can be an effect of competition between the world systems and bind resources.

Having isolated revolutions in backward countries can only be successful in the long run if they are followed by revolutions in the centers of world economy, the most industrialized countries. Real democracy cannot be exercised in protected, limited areas, as in the Soviet Union or China, but needs to be realized globally to work. This is where the question of nationalism and internationalism comes into play.

4.14. The Role of universal Suffrage

In the Western world, universal suffrage is a very central and important part of our political and institutional understanding of democracy. Within capitalism, it is not possible to question the system with all its institutions itself. The owners of the means of production enforce their interests politically. They will use all legitimate means possible within the framework of the political system in order to do so - for example, capitalists fund research institutes to compose reports with results in their interests. In Brussels and Washington D.C. et al., they have a direct influence on institutions of higher education through lobbyists in the institution's bodies, or corrupt politicians with money or indirectly with fake side-job offers which give them or their family a part of the capitalists profit.[117][118]

According to the crisis theory presented by Karl Marx, regularly in history financial and economic crisis are caused by overproduction of goods, which cannot be sold any more. The actual crisis is no exception Actually, there is no political solution to be found to this problem in the west, and no perspective of finding any, it endangers the legitimization of Western democracies. People experience their material status being lowered, while the politicians cannot solve the crisis within the framework of the capitalist system and Western democracy, in which votes are mostly scheduled every four to

---

[117] European Commission: Report from the Commission to the Council and the European Parliament – EU Anti-Corruption Report, Brussels, 03.02.2014; online source: http://ec.europa.eu/dgs/home-affairs/what-we-do/policies/organized-crime-and-human-trafficking/corruption/anti-corruption-report/index_en.htm seen 22.10.2014

[118] Roberts, Dan: Bitter Washington DC mayoral election clouded by corruption claims; The Guardian online, 30.03.2014. online source: http://www.theguardian.com/world/2014/mar/30/washington-dc-mayor-election-corruption-claims seen 22.10.2014

five years. Only once in this period do the ruling party have to bring the constituent to vote for him, or as Marx puts it:

"Instead of deciding once in three or six years which member of the ruling class was to misrepresent the people in Parliament, universal suffrage was to serve the people, constituted in Communes".[119]

Hence, universal suffrage within the framework of capitalism is not a means for true democracy, but limited participation for the electorate that does not follow the purpose of the material emancipation of the people.

How can this process be established?

"It is not a question of whether civil society should exercise legislative power through deputies or through all as individuals. Rather, it is a question of the extension and greatest possible universalization of voting, of active as well as passive suffrage. This is the real point of dispute in the matter of political reform."[120]

In other words, a legislative process must be made possible by

---

[119] Marx, Karl: Civil War in France, Chapter 5: The Paris Commune, 1871; online source: www.marxists.org/archive/marx/works/1871/civil-war-france/ch05.htm seen 07.2013

[120] Marx, Karl: Critique of Hegel's Philosophy of Right, original written: 1843; edition Oxford University Press, 1970, online source: http://www.marxists.org/archive/marx/works/1843/critique-hpr/ch06.htm (7 of 13)

the workers' movements themselves, by communes directly to the biggest extent possible.

Since the new kind of universal suffrage exceeds the existing model through its different form, the content therefore changes too. In socialism, while the old system dies out and a new one comes into existence, universal voting is a regular phenomenon, including forums and rooms for controversial, dynamic discussion both in spoken, as well as in written form, like democratically-led arguments in newspapers. Nowadays, the Internet carries additional potential for a revolution of ideas. All in all, real democracy can be summarized as lively, collective participation, so the social decisions taken after a discussion process, involving the majority of the people are based on this exact disputation of all the people, instead of only some representatives.

As we can see, universal suffrage in Marx's sense is not to be mistaken with the old form of the democratic system. Only all these institutional reforms, or the sum of revolutions inside society according to the arguments mentioned, together with universal suffrage, constitute the circumstances for true democracy. The connection of socialism and true democracy hence becomes obvious.

Next, let's have a look at the connection of suffrage and "people's will".

According to bourgeois ideologists, the universal suffrage should uncover not only the will of status groups and classes, but also the will of the whole of the people. So what does the 'will of the whole of the people' consist of? It consists out of the contradicting 'wills' of all the 'separate status groups and classes'. Capitalism, the will of the people, the will of the majority, is the will not of single status groups and classes, but of a single class, and those other classes which are dependent upon the ruling class industrially and commercially.[121]

So the "ideas of the ruling class are in every epoch the ruling ideas"; this also applies to concept of democracy: the ruler of the economic basis at the same time dominates ideological creation.[122]

---

[121] Marx Engels Werke, Dietz Verlag Berlin, 1970, Vol. 6, German Edition, p. 199-208: "Die Berliner "National-Zeitung" an die Urwähler", Neue Rheinische Zeitung, Nr. 205, 26.01.1849

[122] Marx, Karl: The German Ideology, Part I: Feuerbach. Opposition of the Materialist and Idealist Outlook, part B. The Illusion of the Epoch, chapter: Ruling Class and Ruling Ideas; online source: www.marxists.org/archive/marx/works/1845/german-ideology/ch01b.htm seen 05.06.2014

4.15. Suffrage and True Democracy

We can see that the truth of universal suffrage within the capitalist system is to keep up the masses' support of the system by regular long-term elections. The people are persuaded to rely on more or less trustworthy representatives. Hence, they see no alternative and feel no need to organize in order to articulate their common interests. Therefore, individualization or atomization of society is in the interest of the capitalist.

Within a historical shift, a class power at first merely potentially exceeds the former ruling class power. This is what happened in Europe to the bourgeoisie before they abolished feudalism, when they succeeded in achieving their own freedom by achieving independence from the aristocracy: The potential power of the European bourgeoisie actually exceeded the aristocracy's real power. They implemented the potential of their taking power and transformed it into material power. They were only able to do so because they had first taken control of economic production.

As today, workers' interests in China are generally tolerated and taken care of by the state, but unlike the bourgeoisie in former Europe, they are not in power: The press, the freedom of assembly, the law of association must be freely available to the working class. Those are preconditions for a real worker's movement, which then might take power in their own hands, i.e. establish workers' or true democracy. The working class must first develop class consciousness: from the potential of a class *in* itself, to a class *for* itself.

This is exactly what we can see in China: Democracy is merely brought from above, top-down as a formalism, it is taught to people and can only have a very limited impact as a contribution to emancipation of people. Real democracy can only develop out of the consciousness of the individual and the collective; the bureaucracy could support this transformation of consciousness by supporting democratic initiatives. Mao described this phenomenon as the "mass line": Theory should have the function of developing the practice of people rather then imposing a theoretical, metaphysical construction developed by scientists, financed by the bureaucracy, on society. For real democracy, workers need essential rights to formulate their interests freely and give their ideas material force. This is the way self-enforcement finally becomes possible.

4.16. The Organization of Workers in Socialism

How can the old state turn to a new state and transform all the institutions and agents?

According to the model of the Paris Commune, it was clear to Marx that old state power must be substituted by a new one. This is also the topic of Mao Zedong in his text 'On New Democracy', namely the transformation of the old state (in the industrialized countries: capitalism; in backwards China in the first half of the 20th century: feudalism) into a new state, that

> "the Commune was to be the political form of even the smallest country hamlet, and that in the rural districts the standing army was to be replaced by a national militia, with an extremely short term of service. The rural communities of every district were to administer their common affairs by an assembly of delegates in the central town, and these district assemblies were again to send deputies to the National Delegation in Paris, each delegate to be at any time revocable and bound by the *mandat imperatif* (formal instructions) of his constituents. The few but important functions which would still remain

for a central government were not to be suppressed, as has been intentionally misstated, but were to be discharged by Communal and thereafter responsible agents." [123]

This socialist, democratic state power cannot be imposed artificially by willpower from the outside, as we can see in contemporary history with the U.S. trying to export their model of democracy to various countries with very different economic and historical developments, for instance in the Near East during the Afghanistan and Iraq war. Implementing Western policy. Accordingly, the Chinese authorities deny Western style democracy mechanisms, especially elections and a multi-party system, and a superstructure for China has to find its own path to democracy by holding on to the de facto united party system.

The superstructure, and democracy as a part of the political mechanisms of society, is based on the economic structure. If politicians in a foreign nation try to bring western democracy to an economically backwards country by just constructing those institutions democracy is based on in western countries, and introducing elections, it becomes an artificial process and does not make a non-democratic nation pluralistic. Nor does it

---

[123]   Marx, Karl: Civil War in France, Chapter 5: The Paris Commune, 1871; online source: www.marxists.org/archive/marx/works/1871/civil-war-france/ch05.htm seen 07.2013

increase the people's materialistic wealth, or make them economically well-off. A politician won't make a country democratic at will by superficially changing the political and institutional spheres of a nation. What a representative can do is set the political circumstances *for* the people in such a way that the people themselves can improve their economic basis, the legal system and all of the superstructure. This is a task the workers themselves can do much better and more efficiently on their own, for they know the conditions of production best, as people who shape the world as their profession. In short, democracy cannot be brought about by institutional reforms, but needs to have a revolutionary change of society as its basis, brought about by the people; namely, a democratic, conscious decision of society to transform itself in a revolutionary direction: for example, the case of the Paris Commune's abolition of class society.

The capitalists will mobilize against such an attempt to abolish the basis of their class rule over the workers and they will use their influence on the old state. This class struggle is directly connected with the fight over surplus value: No siphoning of surplus value means no profits, means no basis for the capitalist class's existence.

4.17. The Individual as Part of the Common

Marx made some remarks about the communes according to the example of the commune of Paris. There would be exchanges and coordination on all levels among the communes. In the political context, he did not describe any powerful, centralist superstructure, controlling all the communes and being the highest body as we can see in China nowadays. The political heritage China adopted gradually before and after the revolution of 1949 was so-called 'Marxism-Leninism' through the eyes of Stalin. However, given that there would be some sort of network of communes on an international level, there would be a necessity for communication among local or regional networks. Especially directly after a revolution, such a central organization, i.e. a proletarian state consisting of the monopoly of the proletariat to fulfill tasks formerly fulfilled by the capitalist state, would be necessary, as described before. Its character would orientate directly around the necessities of the majority of the population, i.e. consist of the people and be directly responsible to them.

The unity of the nation was not to be broken, but, on the contrary, to be organized by a Communal Constitution, and become reality by the destruction of the state power which claimed to be the embodiment of that unity, independent of, and superior to, the nation itself, from which it was but a parasitic excrescence. While the merely repressive organs of the old governmental power were to be amputated, its legitimate functions were to be wrested from an authority usurping pre-eminence over society itself, and restored to the responsible agents of society.

The military is the institution for the defense of the state from of mainly foreign, but also internal dangers in order to keep up the established system. The character of the old system differs from the character of the new one.

> "The first decree of the Commune (...) was the suppression of the [old, note] standing army, and the substitution for it of the armed people." [124]

This is how the monopoly on the use of ultimate force is shifted from an elite, professional core, which can easily follow a minority, to the broader masses., The people, therefore, are in

---

[124] Marx, Karl: Selected Works of Karl Marx, 1943 chapter: The Paris Commune, Address to the International Workingmen's Association, May 1871; p. 62

person the ultimate, collective executive. The majority of the people itself then defend the form of the new state, the commune system. The monopoly on the legitimate use of force is abolished by being generalized, as the state in general is abolished by being generalized. The accomplishment of this task can be described as a strong act of democracy, the rule and self-determination of the collective, of the people.

> "With the standing army and the governmental police, the physical force of repression was to be broken" [125]

and

> "governmental force of repression and authority over society was thus to be broken in its merely repressive organs, and where it had legitimate functions to fulfill, these functions were not to be exercised by a body superior to the society, but by the responsible agents of society itself",[126]

with a very short time of service.

---

[125] Marx: The Civil War in France, Second Draft, chapter 2: The Commune, online source: http://www.marxists.org/archive/marx/works/1871/civil-war-france/drafts/ch02.htm

[126] Ibid.

4.18. Idealism and Metaphysics

"In democracy the formal principle is simultaneously the material principle. For that reason it is the first true unity of the universal and the particular."[127]

This transformation of unity between the universal and the particular will take place when "in true democracy the political state disappears." [128]

In Hegel's idealistic view, in class society, a universal class - i.e. the bureaucracy - would bring about the liberation of man from class to realize himself politically, while Marx stresses that universality can only be meaningful if it applies to all classes, not just one.[129]

In Marx's sense, the universal class are the people generally, without the bureaucracy as a superficial class to free them. True democracy is defined by Marx as classless, devoid of private property, and stateless. All throughout history, political

---

[127] Marx: Critique of Hegel's Philosophy of Right, Cambridge University Press 1843; edition 1970, Part 2: The Constitution §§ 272 – 286, chapter: Democracy; online source: http://www.marxists.org/archive/marx/works/1843/critique-hpr/ch02.htm

[128] Ibid.

[129] Quoted according to Avineri, p.35

classes would transform into social classes, therefore they are in the position that "the individual members of a people are equal in the heaven of their political world yet unequal in the earthly existence of society."[130]

So the class that dominates the economic basis is closely connected with the superstructure. Only the free creation of the producer, i.e. the worker, on a collective basis, leads to the free creation of the superstructure through its universalization, its collectivization. In this sense, the personal division between material production and mental production is abolished, or, as Marx calls it, the abolition of the separation between manual and mental work.

The working class does not have freedom of speech and is systematically held back from conquering power. The bourgeoisie influences institutions and seeks to expend this influence with the purpose of spreading their own ideas among the people. Those old social laws still exist and are used against the workers every day. The workers do not have the possibility to let their own representatives, who were selected out of the middle of the workers, speak for them, and they have to rely on

---

[130] Marx, Karl: Critique of Hegel's Philosophy of Right, 1843, Chapter 5, online source: www.marxists.org/archive/marx/works/1843/critique-hpr/ch05.htm seen 11.11.2014

other elements; during Marx's life this was the known as the radical petty bourgeoisie[131], nowadays in China it is the CCP (the question of the class composition of the CCP will not be dealt with in this paper).

4.19. A Federation of Soviets for Coordination

We have discussed the question of representation and specialization in policy-making and universal suffrage on an abstract level. In which way can those principles work on a concrete, geographical basis nationwide, or even internationally, if a revolution spreads and national borders fall, and the proletariat rules in a number of countries?

First, to establish communism it is crucial to keep following the principle of internationalism and solidarity. National and internationally the unity and formation of the workers' movement is, for the present, completely restricted in practice, that means it is hard for activists to establish a strong, united movement which can potentially take power. Active solidarity is nationally and internationally necessary, for "The working

---

[131] Marx Engels Werke, Dietz Verlag Berlin, 1975, Vol. 6, p.559

men have no country", as Marx writes in the Communist Manifesto[132]. The workers movement faces difficulties in building grass root structures outside the party, namely NGOs, which find it hard to promote worker's empowerment as a class. In Germany, Marx founded in worker's societies for the education of workers with the goal of promoting worker's empowerment on the principle of solidarity and internationalism.[133]

In a historic example, Engels pointed out in 1875 that even though the German working class initially constituted their power within the state borders, i.e. nationally, it was actually aware of the solidarity of the workers all over the world and would be prepared to fulfill their duty of solidarity; for example, helping and supporting strikes.[134] The organized working class in China is advised to follow this appeal of international solidarity, as the international proletariat is

---

[132] Marx, Engels: Manifesto of the Communist Party, 1848, Chapter 2. online source: www.marxists.org/archive/marx/works/1848/communist-manifesto/ch02.htm

[133] Garcia, Magaly Rodriguez: Early Views on Internationalism: Marxist Socialists vs Liberals, in Revue belge de philologie et d'histoire, 2006, Vol. 84, Nr. 84-4, p. 1061-1062. online source: http://www.persee.fr/web/revues/home/prescript/article/rbph_0035-0818_2006_num_84_4_5060?_Prescripts_Search_tabs1=standard&_ seen 20.12.2014

[134] Engels to August Beel in Zwickau, London, 18./28.03.1875 (letter). Marx Engels Werke, Dietz Verlag Berlin, 1975, Vol. 34, p. 126

constrained to do so, even though their first priority is to seize power in their countries.

Solidarity does not stop at state borders but it is a key value of communism and a practical tool for the working class to live their lives as social beings. It means standing together in times of problems and suffering, as well as supporting the fight for emancipation. In a general context, it means identifying the particular problems of society as general problems of the human species and the search for a common solution, i.e. the stronger and further developed supporting the weaker, more backwards (country, worker, group etc.).

During the civil war in France, the uprising working class of the Paris Commune had to defend themselves against the repression of the old state power to create free associations internationally.

"The Communal Constitution has been mistaken for an attempt to break up into the federation of small states, (...) that unity of great nations which, if originally brought about by political force, has now become a powerful coefficient of social production. The antagonism of the Commune against the state power has been mistaken for an exaggerated form of the ancient struggle against over-centralization."

and

> "The Paris Commune was, of course, to serve as a model to all the great industrial centers of France. The communal regime once established in Paris and the secondary centers, the old centralized government would in the provinces, too, have to give way to the self-government of the producers."[135]

With the goal of true democracy at stake, the working class has the power in hand to end the struggle of the capitalist class against the working class and vice versa by abolishing the capitalist class, by dissolving it, by changing the privileged status of this minority to that one no different of the majority of people. In this state of political equality, true democracy in a network of communes on the basis of freedom is possible. Barriers and borders as a sign of separation become, with the collective rule of one class with the same interests, redundant; the same is true of racism, sexism, homophobia and other means of marginalization.

In isolation, China as a single country cannot succeed in establishing real democracy in one, economically backwards

---

[135] Marx, Karl: Civil War in France, Chapter 5: The Paris Commune, 1871; online source: www.marxists.org/archive/marx/works/1871/civil-war-france/ch05.htm

country. It will need the help of the industrialized West, which is not foreseeable in the short term.

As long as confrontation between the systems continues, there will be no real democracy in China. Internationalism is a crucial criterion for true democracy in the long term.

The fate of workers' democracy in China goes hand in hand with the development of workers' democracy internationally, especially with the situation in the developed countries of the West. Indicators for the development of true democracy in China are the international development of the economy and the finance crisis of the capitalist system on the one hand, and the establishment of consciousness among workers to organize themselves on the basis of solidarity on the other. At the moment, capitalists internationally are tending to take further advantage of the crisis. They use it for a redistribution of wealth in society to keep their profits, while the losses are limited to the material situation of the working class.

5. Conclusion: Merging of Marx's Democracy and China's Democracy Debate

5.1. History and Theory

Theoretically, following Marx bibliographical development, he started in his youth being a radical pro-democrat, but concluded in his later development that democracy can and should be in its original sense the rule of the *majority* people, which are those suppressed in the capitalist system: This interpretation he calls real democracy, that he interprets in the most radical sense, i.e. the most direct rule of the people possible in industrialized countries.

In reality, most nations experienced a phase of radical democracy, but the permanent establishment of communism in its original sense, i.e. national decision making on the basis of communes taking the commune of Paris as an orientation, only succeeded in the short run. Historically, they were mainly small minorities in a country, for instance Paris against the capitalist rule of France, or a small nation, for example Cuba against their historical main enemy, the U.S., where the state power sought to establish real democracy according to Marx's theoretically analyzed examples and theoretical works. Only the Soviet Union and China succeeded in following the path towards true democracy in a territory and with enough people and resources to establish an economy, and not vulnerable enough to fall to attacks by the capitalist, pre-dominant powers. Obviously, the Soviet Union fell, while China struggles with its version of democracy, which had already changed from Marx to the Soviet Union, and then went through further changes up to now. Mao made many theoretical concessions to the Soviet Union, and, especially after the exclusion of Chen Duxiu from the party in 1927, the character of the discussion about democracy was transformed from a definition of democracy as "the rule of the majority" to "democracy as the rule of bureaucracy on behalf of the people", including a farcical debate about how to improve the representatives' loyalty to the people. Out of these complex relations we can explain that the term 'democracy' is dealt with very carefully, because it bears the seed of revolution.

Concerning the topic of true democracy, we can talk about the contradictory role of the CP. Rhetorically, the CCP as the political elite leans on its communist roots for its legitimization, i.e. on Marx and Mao as the most important philosophers for a hybrid system of Stalinist representative democracy, including Western influences with elements from the Maoist era. In the articles of the People's Daily, the party communicates problems and issues to the public and tries to popularize its own interpretation of democracy. However, the very term democracy is not interpreted in its original, direct democratic sense according to the ancient Greeks or Marx, but comes from a degenerated interpretation of the "dictatorship of the proletariat" (see chapter: The Question of Representation, p. 63).

The Chinese interpretation rhetorically includes, but actually physically excludes the proletariat in its decision-making process, and interprets democracy as the CCP's "rule on behalf of the people".

Decisive elements are bureaucrats who depend on the expertise of scientists in their service.

On the one hand, in the upper middle layer we can see progressive intellectuals, i.e. reformists, who seek to win this and that little victory for formal, petty bourgeois democratic requests, for this or that democratic reform.

On the other hand, the Chinese leadership seeks to balance its power on the edge between capitalism and a state-planned economy, while drifting increasingly towards the globally predominant system of capitalism. The self-appointed representatives of the people are trapped between loyalty to the interests of the capitalists, which is connected with the bureaucracy on the one side, and the class struggle of progressive elements of the working class on the other.

Here, the economic situation plays an important role for class struggle.

The extending capitalist relations of production promote the development of productive forces for a time, but gradually change to become chains on economic and social development. The potential of production cannot be seized, because the capitalist form of ownership does not allow it. At a certain point, depending on their level of consciousness, the productive classes try to change the relation of production according to their own interests. The ruling class will mobilize means of suppression, which might lead the class struggle into a revolutionary phase. In this democratic revolution, the long-suppressed classes seize power and reshuffle the ownership structure in their favor.

Methodically, this revolutionary theory is created out of the practice of human life; it abstracts facts and experiences in order to promote the practice of man, namely economical, technological, political and cultural production. The only aim of theory is to improve this practice. If it does not fulfill this purpose, that theory is useless for humanity, because it detaches from human practice, from human life.

Rhetorically, the CCP is pro-democracy; practically it's not interested in promoting the liberation of the working class because it fears the consequences of its emancipation and self-determination, such as losing its privileged position in society.

Because the global economic crisis has slowed down industrialized countries' economic power to almost a standstill and historically slowly brings their historically promoted, political system of capitalism, based on bourgeois democracy, there might be a chance for a scope for freedom to leap forward in history to a new, democratic revolution for the workers internationally and in China to shift the economic power they possess in their role in the production process back into their own hands and become not only the 'masters in their own affairs' in theory, as the CCP promotes in the People, but also in practice. So an integral part of a truly democratic revolution could be for the working people of China to abolish the state and dissolve its structure and functions in themselves according to the principles Marx analyzed in several writings, including "The Civil War in France".[136]

The CCP has a certain interest in economic growth in order to maintain stability; to achieve this goal, the CCP can take two paths.

For the purpose of maintaining stability, the CCP has a strong interest in expanding the economy. As a general principle, the growth of the economic sector satisfies the privileged classes, namely the capitalists' and certain parts of the bureaucracy's wealth, accumulated from the surplus labor of the working class. At the same time, the CCP has to guarantee relative stability between the classes relating to the share of surplus for the working class. In times of economic crisis the economic growth rate has to remain comparably high compared to the

---

[136] Marx, Karl: The Civil War in France; The Third Address; May, 1871, Chapter The Paris Commune,
online source: www.marxists.org/archive/marx/works/1871/civil-war-france/ch05.htm, seen 07.2013

pre-crisis period. Otherwise, the proportion of the growth profits for capitalists and the growth of materialistic wealth of working class through wage labor are thrown out of balance.

If there is not enough profit left to guarantee at least some growth to the workers in order to provide a certain rise in living standards and satisfy their needs, while the suppressor acquires the bigger part of the surplus labor for themselves, the question of political instability is out of the CP's control. An organized workers movement challenging the regime would be the start of the establishment of true democracy.

In conclusion, the CP, a caste tending to structurally favor the capitalist class, fails to draw the right conclusions, out of an analysis of political economy, in favoring the working class and handing actual control of the means of production over to the working class. Theoretical links to the working class remain a relic from the past, while modern policy-making does not take the workers as the center of attention, either in theory, or in practice (see, for example, migrant workers).

Also, in order to translate a model of democratic control according to the Marx's analysis, the party has to organize the workers, and society as a whole, for the purpose of governing and controlling the means of production, so that individuals can produce according to their needs and not to serve a minority with their surplus labor; that their free time is disposable, allowing them to consume for non-productive purposes, like science, research, art, organization of society, etc.

The CCP's willingness to bring about profound, democratic reforms in a Marxist sense, i.e. shifting power from the bureaucracy to the workers, either in reforms, or in a revolution, and thereby promote the emancipation of workers and society as a whole, is limited.

The CP, as a privileged caste in society, is, in the final analysis, the main and decisive factor concerning the superstructure of Chinese society. Its role is much more one of a dictatorship *for* the people than a dictatorship *of* the people. The "People's Republic" in China's official name "People's Republic of China" was created by loyalists of Stalinist communism, which actually seems to refer to the capitalist class more than to the interests of the workers and peasants, who created the state during the civil war, with their revolution against a corrupt regime.

On a theoretical level, we can find a central, international, historical debate among revolutionaries who refer to Marx; namely, is it possible to carry out a successful long-term revolution within a nation where the means of production are not yet fully developed? In other words, is a revolution in an economically backwards country possible, or does an industrialized country have to undergo a real democratic revolution first, before suppressed nations can follow?

Lenin and Mao put the theoretical model of socialism into practice on a national scale and in two economically backwards countries for the first time in history. While Lenin answered the question positively - since in Tsarist Russia before 1917 the masses were suppressed and the conditions for revolution more than ripe - Mao planned to establish "New Democracy" as a stage between semi-feudalism and socialism, whereby Chinese capitalism would cooperate with the socialist state. This position was adopted by Mao's successors and is still, or again, to be found in party documents today.[137] This theoretical debate was historically already carried out in Russia around 1917, on the one hand among Mensheviks and Bolsheviks, and on the other in China before 1949; namely, if a feudal or half-feudal

---

[137] CCP: Constitution of Communist Party of China, Adopted on Nov. 14, 2012, online source: http://www.china.org.cn/china/18th_CCP_congress/2012-11/16/content_27138030.htm, seen 25.01.2013

county with a weak proletariat need first establish capitalism to improve its economy in order to create the means of production in a backwards country, before it can start to introduce communism, or if workers' democracy can be established in a backwards country directly. Here, backwardness does not only describe the economic state of development, but also the cultural one. In short, is it necessary for China to go through capitalism, as Deng Xiaoping proposed, or is it possible to create communism, and along with it "real democracy", in one country, as Stalin suggested after Lenin passed away?

China decided to go neither of the suggested paths, but opened and continuously and slowly opens up the economy to capitalist countries, while keeping up the political rule of the one party system to control these influences.

This leads us to the phenomenon of Bonapartism, i.e. a political rule in society which resembles that one of the Bonapartes: a military dictator rules. Marx described this phenomenon in the beginning of the first chapter of "The Eighteenth Brumaire of Louis Bonaparte" 1852 as the "rule by the sword": in a situation, where no class is able to take power in society, a self-announced leader might appear in a revolutionary situation and take over the movement, leaning on the mass movement in a specific, historical situation, and use it for his own purposes. By doing that, a regime might be temporarily established without any connection to the masses.

However, in the end, class relations decide the rule of society: In China, bureaucratically regulated capitalism still extends the working class' power, so the working class cannot rule on its own, or in other words, the CCP rules behalf of the people. The contradictions in society are accumulating, along with the profit of Chinese capitalists, and the means of suppression against the working class movements as class struggles are growing, and becoming more sophisticated and complex: Direct violent suppression is substituted by indirect media propaganda, accompanied by anti-terrorist actions, orientated around Western techniques.[138] [139]

---

[138] Riegler, Thomas: Terrorismus. Akteure, Strukturen, Entwicklungslinien; Studien Verlag 2009, Innsbruck;

[139] Göbel, Christian, Ong, Lynette H., 2012, Social Unrest in China, Europe China Research and Advice Network, online source: http://www.euecran.eu/Long%20Papers/ECRAN%20Social%20Unrest%20in%20China_%20Christian%20Gobel%20and%20Lynette%20H.%20Ong.pdf seen 03.11.2014

In the Chinese discussion, this scientific democracy has a very different connotation. It is based on the expertise of consultants in think tanks, financed by the CP. In this closed model of the education and the policy makers, the majority of the population is excluded. This is a farce of a democratic system.[140] Generally spoken, democracy has nothing to do with an apparatus of experts, it is rather monarchy which relies on an apparatus of ministers and experts, ruling on behalf of the people. The purpose of democracy is to avoid abuse of power; no matter the level of expertise, it should merely be a consulting element for the forum of citizens, which exercises policy more or less directly. In this progress, the expert has no more or less power than other individuals, but can convince others within dialogue with arguments in his field of expertise.

There is a gap between the CCP bureaucracy and the masses, which the CCP is well aware of. The Mao Zedong Ideas, which constitute an important, theoretical fundament of party ideology, were theories aimed at overcoming this gap, and linking the bureaucracy with the masses, or in Marx's words, making representatives agents of the people: According to the "mass line" of Mao, ideas of the masses should be adopted as a

---

[140] 何聪　朱磊：深化政务公开　凸显科学民主　安徽：行政决策"敞开门"，2011.11.30

general theory, theorized on this higher level, and then brought back to the masses, whereby the people would recognize these ideas as their generalized interests, their own ideas on a higher level. This philosophical relict degenerated, as explained in this paper.

Nowadays, the degenerated practice of the CCP could be summarized in a Bonapartist way:

(1) The CCP adopts ideas of the masses.

(2) The CCP includes their interests, including the interests of capitalists.

(3) The CCP popularizes these compromises between the interests of the working class on the one side with their own, bureaucratic interests, including those of capitalists.

The state is not led by the people, but *on behalf* of the people by a caste. The CCP rules with the tolerance of the proletariat, rather than supporting its interests.

5.2. The actual Situation

Let's move away from history and theory and turn to the actual process of policy-making. In the representation of the dictatorship of the proletariat, there is a blindness for sociopolitical relations inside society; for example, migrant workers are still a marginalized group, facing long-term prejudice from citizens in big cities, who cannot settle down at their working place. This kind of discrimination we could compare with the phenomenon of racism against migrant workers from economically backward countries, which takes place in western countries. Generally, democratic reforms are mainly top-down, the toleration and official support of democratic bottom-up articulation is hardly happening - this is a very obvious consequence of the perception of representative democracy without democratic control of marginalized groups.

Moreover, according to recent tendencies, the acceptance of capitalist representatives inside the party grows, which destroys hopes for a positive, future role of the CCP as an advocate for emancipation for the working class. Up to now, the CCP's approach towards emancipation has been merely economical and not political, and there are few signs that this might change. There are indeed ongoing debates about democracy, but the direction of those are about small reforms or positive, minority examples. This suggests that the CCP wants to keep the proletariat calm rather than inspire and motivate it to seize state power and dissolve the state within the class.

What does economic democracy mean for China's democratic situation? Since the start of the crisis, China's GDP has not increased, staying around 10%, as it was in the pre-crisis years until 2011, but went back to a level of 7.7% in 2013.[141] This is still an extremely high rate compared to the stagnating economic rate of the western world. However, the economy is still going down, while the level of class struggle goes up. The discrepancy within the bureaucracy balancing between the interests of capitalists and the people, is becoming more severe. Even though the nationalized, planned sector of economy within the Chinese economy is an important pillar, controlling key industries, the income gap between the minority of capitalist and the majority of workers and peasants is getting bigger. The reaction of the CCP in the years of crisis was a shift away from an export-orientated economy to a nationwide orientated economy, increasingly under capitalist control.

In China, inner party democracy and communication between the party and the people are strictly separated. The former underlies a strict party discipline and citizens standing outside the party bureaucracy especially argue about the bureaucracy,

---

[141] World Bank,
http://data.worldbank.org/indicator/NY.GDP.MKTP.KD.ZG
seen 02.10.2014

whose members partly consider themselves an exclusive elite. Democratic centralism is merely mentioned by Marx indirectly, only later was it theoretically developed by Lenin as a state model or form of state, degenerated by war and isolation in the backwards country and later exported from the Stalinist Soviet Union to the People's Republic of China. The Chinese state constructed the People's Congresses as the Chinese version of a special form of Stalinist democratic centralism, for party intern democracy: Party unity and discipline of the lower layers of the system plays a more important role than in the Leninist model. Democracy outside the party concentrates on communication, with the purpose of bringing politicians together with the people they rule, including the improvement of communication on a verbal and written basis, finding out about people's problems and promoting people's adoption of the party's opinion.

Democracy is seen by the CCP as having the potential to harmonize contradictions between people and politicians and is controlled from above. Decision-making is done for the people, not of the people.

One general, important character trait of Chinese society is that they are more of a collective society, rather than an individualized, which has influences on the culture of discussion, for example, one is not supposed to directly criticize his superior, a qualified boss must rather know about the problems of their subjects. This quite trivial fact has severe consequences for the perception of democracy: The discourse about democracy in China remains quite vague, general and theoretical, while Marx's critiques are most direct and concrete. In the Chinese discussion, theory prevails over practical instructions. Also, analysis of the general, overall situation of democracy in China hardly exists, as with researches or broad empirical studies. In the material researched on, we can find merely a few positive examples of how the CCP imagines democracy, and we can therefore conclude that the balance of power inside the decisive party organs are generally against those in favor of truly democratic reform.

So, will there be a slow, reformist approach towards an emancipated society in China?

Democracy in China, as participation of the people in governmental and state affairs, is a vehicle to improve the existent system of governance and hardly preserves people's interests. It is a tool for the bureaucracy to continue rule on behalf of the people and preserve their privileges. A potential turn towards this kind of policy, i.e. the usage of democracy as a tool for people's interests, for self-governance, including discussions among people and deputies on an equal basis, is still far away – progressive agents inside the CCP are a minority.

However, Marx described, as a historical materialist law, how the bigger the dimension of the proletariat the more possible is the chance for a shift of power in favor of the proletariat, because the power proportions of the proletariat in relation to the capitalist change in the proletariat's favor. At an uncertain point, depending on class consciousness, where the economic growth in society produces enough proletarians, quantity turns to quality: The workers and suppressed class under capitalism take matters into their own hands. The course of such an event would take place in a dialectical rather than a gradual way, namely because it is contradictory.

Naturally, history does not repeat itself identically, and also we cannot just lean back and wait for injustices to fall automatically because of such a tendency, as described by Marx, but we must learn from history to grow on it and improve our practice today by studying historical developments of the past.

Since historical developments have similarities, but differ in other points, a potential Chinese revolution would not imitate or copy the past one by one, although it will have parallels with developments of the past. An aware proletariat would certainly have to learn from historic examples in order to be successful over a long period of time. From Marx's analysis of the commune of Paris, future Chinese revolutionaries might learn, for instance, that in order to establish true democracy,- The education system must be open to the public, whereby potential and talent must be the criteria for advancement of pupils rather than class affiliation.- The standing military must be substituted by the armed people, following the overall dissolution of the state. The time of service should be "extremely short", so the army would not become an independent power, but on the contrary be almost identical with the masses.- The socialization of production, i.e. the key industries, can be started by the workers, with a tight connection to society, which is the fundament for true democracy in micro, as well as macro-structures all through society. This way, the workers exceed their modern role in capitalist society as mere tools, so-called human resources, and become creators of their own material, human world.

In China today, micro groups do not exist as a vivid basis for discussions by the working class, while small communes are a legacy from the past and exist out of economic necessity. They do not have rights to freely elected "communal agents", but rather prefer a hierarchically centralized caste on a macro basis. Within the party structure, democracy is established to a certain degree, however, due to the political structure's impermeability and exclusiveness *not* focusing on the working class personally and on their needs and purposes. From the issue of education and the military, and the effective organization of the working class, ultimately the focus does not lie unconditionally on the emancipation of the working class. Even though the CCP succeeds in a way to fulfill the task of improving the working class in a quantitative matter, qualitatively there is no leap to worker's emancipation, the centerpiece of Marx's terminology of true democracy.

Merely speaking of democracy without a connection to practice, or merely being a scratch word with purely intellectual definition, democracy may only be interpreted by the think-tanks of the CP, namely universities, academies and other intellectual circles under the predominance of the CP. Such an approach is purely theoretical and therefore, as Marx criticized Hegel, metaphysics.

The CCP has ongoing debates about democratic reforms. The discussions are merely formalist and general. Up to now, no implementation of these reforms has been taken. The multi-party system with the democratic parties in China, and the consultative conferences taking place regularly are more of an alibi than proof of true democracy in China. In practice, the CCP contradicts the arguments of a minority inside the party in favor of democratic reforms: Situations like during the Cultural Revolution could come up. They speak out warnings about different fractions inside the CCP that could split and fight each other in a violent way, which could go as far as civil war. I want to draw a parallel to the U.S., which uses a method with similar arguments against the political enemy: An atmosphere of fear, of an artificial threat, is created and spread by media with the purpose of stabilizing society. The nation as an abstract, political union must be defended against threatening elements, whose only purpose seems to be to destroy the lives of innocent people. An alien danger is created, so individuals favor their actual situation compared to unknown risks they might take when trying to change the status quo. This trick is nothing else than the distraction of people, it relies on the psychological principle that fears are emotionally stronger than hopes in a society.[142] Back to the example of China, a strong and unified state will misuse people's trust for their own purposes and to hide their own problems. The topic of terrorism, an inner or outer enemy endangering the state's stability, leads China to ally with Western countries.

To give a concrete example, some Xinjiang Uigures feel they are treated as potential terrorists rather than fellow citizens that the CCP representatives listen to and cooperate with in solidarity. This is a severe, democratic issue.

Practical theory must have the role of improving practice; hence, it must be rooted in practice. If theory is merely created by unproductive forces in society, which the elites of the CCP are, theoretical terms and debates may loose their practical connotation. Words, which describe a concrete problem, relation or condition turn to terms without practical meaning, to a subject useful for debates and discourses, but useless for the improvement of practice of humanity, i.e. problems of the human species.

---

[142] Riegler, Thomas: Terrorismus Akteure, Strukturen, Entwicklungslinien, Studien Verlag Österreich 2009

Generally speaking, a societies' developments and innovations are closely connected to a society's ability to combine theory and practice, guaranteeing the solution of this society's problems. Often, regulations in a society need to be changed to be solved, for example there are ongoing, public discussions in the media about migration, generally from economically poorer regions to economically developed regions, for instance from Africa to the EU, from Mexico to the US or from the rural areas to the coastal areas in China. gives way to economic, intellectual and cultural advancement of society.

Consequently, the inclusion of the masses as 'practitioners' in theory, i.e. debates in public forums orally (public discussions) or by writing (the newspaper, magazines, online forums) is the ultimate necessity for true democracy according to Marx. In present day China, the discussion forum of the newspaper People's Daily is a party organ for popularization of solutions the party found for societies problems, or in other words, it's a party organ where experts analyze society and draw their conclusions, not an organ working people can discuss about their fertile ideas to create their own society, as described in Marxist works.

In his view, the overall majority of the people and the proletariat as the most creative element in a society in general and China in this case, are the pillars of economy. They have the potential and the ability to ultimately decide over the nation's fate. The intellectual support of them, the study of historical experiences in real democracy and systematic education with the goal of the creation of the acknowledgment within the proletariat of this role, might promote the creation of a class for itself, i.e. help the working class taking power. To make a small contribution is to this process is the concrete purpose of this Master-thesis.

By the argumentation given, we can describe the character of the bureaucracy established in China. Like every representative under the influence of capitalism, it has turned away from the working class to merely represent it. In a historic process of specialization and the return of ancient traditions of administration, the purpose of the working class differs from those of the bureaucracy, so the representatives are alienated from the working class. Traditionally, a bureaucrat's prime interests are positive relations to other bureaucrats of the same rank and the upper rank to speed up their carrier, so they can hope for promotion.

The CCP's conception of democracy has much in common with the points Marx criticized about Bakunin, including the abolition of the hereditary rights, the equality of class differences (merely by definition) and the request that the working class is not allowed to get involved in politics, though it may organize in trade unions. (see page 51, chapter: Idealism and Materialism: Marx and Bakunin). These are remarkable parallels to China's policy: Therefore we can assume that the CCP is not a worker's organization, but it is detached from the working class basis. For example migrant workers have no real representation – a problem which is mentioned in the People's Daily and which the party at least rhetorically seeks to correct. As long as workers mainly join the party for careerist reasons and not because of the motivation for improving the situation of their class, the proletariat is individualized and isolated and cannot improve their own, material condition. The CCP as the political elite indirectly contributes to the collectivization of the working class, which is a side effect of the process of opening China towards capitalism. The working class in China is a class in itself and the CCP contributes to preventing its development as a class *for* itself. It prevents a real democratic process of collectivization, the rise of the class's collective material condition and their political emancipation. The working class has to fulfill this task itself by the means of class struggle.

5.3. The Question of a democratic Revolution

The economic goal of a truly democratic society is an economic system orientated around the exchangeable value of products, which is about the price of a product, to practical value. That means a democratically planned economy deciding on the quantity and quality of products, rather than a capitalist market. A democratically planned market orientates itself around what people need, rather than how much profit the owner of the means of production can accumulate from the goods he produces.

In China, the national economy is still being developed under the combination of capitalist and planned influences of the state. Therefore, this hybrid system of production between capitalism and a planned economy is still able to achieve high GDP growth rates. Only if a system can no longer satisfy society's needs, is the historic necessity created for its replacement by a new one. China's economy is developing well, despite the global economic crisis, therefore the bureaucracy can still give a growing part of the surplus value to workers and the materialistic needs of workers can be satisfied to a growing extent. So I consider the scenario of a real democratic revolution, i.e. an overthrow of the government by a popular uprising of the Chinese people, as extremely unlikely within the next few years.

I am convinced that in order to reach real democracy by *either* a revolutionary overthrow in the long run *or* by wide-ranging reforms, driven by class struggles as an expression of the organized working class, the active support of a real democratic, industrially developed country would be necessary. That means that the revolutionary process must be part of a real ongoing, international democratic revolution, including active solidarity among countries. An example of solidarity between countries can be seen in the 1950s: The rapid industrialization of China after 1949 was only possible because of technology transfer from the Soviet Union in the first years. The economic potential of China was materialized by this help, but today is still far from being fully developed, due to a lack of possibilities in democratic participation for the majority on matters of their daily life, especially production and distribution.

In this sense, a sustainable reorganization of society, or in other words a long lasting, democratic revolution in favor of the proletariat and at the expense of capitalists and the state apparatus, would be strongly dependent on the support of a revolutionary process in the developed world. An isolated, backwards country is not able to compete with a hostile, capitalist outer world in the long run, even if planning mechanisms are more efficient and even if it was as big as China, according to the lesson learned during the Cultural Revolution.

The ancient Chinese middle kingdom did not have much of a democratic tradition before the republican era. A democratic tradition is constructed as an expression of historic necessity; for example, Western democracies relate to ancient Greece and the democratic approach was popularized by philosophers of the enlightenment in Europe, historic events never experienced by Chinese philosophers and people.

The specific historic development of China is in many aspects unique from that of Europe and the US, and accordingly must have a unique democratic approach.

In China's communist party, there are indeed still Marxists. There are true democrats in a Marxist sense inside the party. They are still a minority and in a defensive position. However, as soon as the level of class struggle with a wide political, emancipatory program - i.e. the struggle for true democracy and communism in Marx's definition - rises, those elements might be able to once again adopt an offensive position, on the back of these struggles, because they know the system, they know its mistakes and they know how to change it for the well-being of society. Consequently, a political revolution, a substitution of corrupt and parasitical elements, together with the continuation of the CCP as a party in another form are no contradiction, but the most realistic path. This future will be a new future, not an imitation of the political system of another, small country. With its dimension of territory, resources and people, we can expect the Chinese proletariat to learn from mistakes made by the bourgeois political leaders in the most developed parts of the world. A future according to Marx's philosophy must be without today's representatives and without an indirect form of democracy, as seen in the democratic model of Europe and the US.

The people will use the method of historical materialism to build their own, truly democratic future. The process can be made possible with and through the unity of the working people all around the world. Therefore, Marx concluded the "Manifesto" with the words:

The proletarians have nothing to lose but their chains. They have a world to win. Proletarians of all countries, unite! [143]

---

[143] Karl Marx's last sentence in the famous Communist Manifesto (written together with Frederik Engels), as well as in the opening speech at the founding conference of the first internationale, written between 21 and 27 October 1864, in Marx Engels Werke, Dietz Verlag Berlin, DDR 1968, Vol. 16, p. 5-13;
online source: http://www.marxists.org/deutsch/archiv/marx-engels/1864/10/inaugadr.htm

Bibliography

Avineri, Shromo: The Social and Political Thought of Karl Marx. Cambridge University Press, London, 1968, chapter "True Democracy" p. 31-41

Böke, Henning: Maoismus: China und die Linke - Bilanz und Perspektive, Schmetterling Verlag, Stuttgart, 2007

Buckley, Chris: China Warns Against 'Western Values' in Imported Textbooks, The New York Times, 30.01.2015
http://sinosphere.blogs.nytimes.com/2015/01/30/china-warns-against-western-values-in-imported-textbooks/?_r=0
seen 10.02.2015

CCCCP: Decision of the CCCCP on Some Major Issues Concerning Comprehensively Deepening the Reform, Beijing, China.org.cn, 2014.01.17, VIII. Strengthening Building of the Socialist Democratic System, http://www.china.org.cn/chinese/2014-01/17/content_31226494_8.htm seen 19.05.2014
(corresponding Chinese source:中共中央关于全面深化改革若干重大问题的决定（全文）八、加强社会主义民主政治制度建设 online source: http://www.china.com.cn/news/2013-11/15/content_30615132_4.htm seen 12.01.2015)

China Daily (人民日报 Renmin Ribao) 光盘版 电子版，北京, 人民网版权所有. The archive of the years used between 2009-2011 is available online:
search.people.com.cn/rmw/GB/bkzzsearch/index.jsp
China Economic Review: Banking reform: China bets on privatization to save village banks, China Economic Review, 29.07.2013, online source:
http://www.chinaeconomicreview.com/rural-banks-banking-private-ownership-privatized-SME-BOC-regulation seen 22.10.2014

China Internet Information Center, Beijing:
http://www.china.org.cn/english/archiveen/27743.htm and
http://www.china.org.cn/english/Political/26144.htm seen 10.05.2014

CCP: Constitution of Communist Party of China, Adopted on Nov.
14, 2012
online source:
http://www.china.org.cn/china/18th_CCP_congress/2012-
11/16/content_27138030.htm seen 01.2013

Ehmer, Philipp: Strukturwandel in China, Deutsche Bank Research,
Frankfurt, Germany, 2011, p.2. online resource:
http://www.dbresearch.de/PROD/DBR_INTERNET_DE-
PROD/PROD0000000000269158.pdf seen 29.10.2014

Feigon, Lee: Mao: A Reinterpretation, 2003, Ivan R. Dee, Chicago

Grant, Ted: History of British Trotskysm, Well Red Books, London
2002

Hornby, Lucy: China lets Gini out of the bottle; wide wealth gap,
Reuters. Online source:
http://www.reuters.com/article/2013/01/18/us-china-economy-
income-gap-idUSBRE90H06L20130118 seen 10.10.2014

Hunt, Alan: Marxism and Democracy, London: Lawrence & Wishart
Ltd, 1980, p. 76

Institut für Marxismus-Leninismus beim ZK der SED: Karl Marx –
Friedrich Engels Werke, Sachregister (for edition 1–39). Dietz
Verlag, Berlin, 1989; keyword: Demokratie, p. 144-145
online source:
http://marxwirklichstudieren.files.wordpress.com/2012/11/mew_sach
register-1989-dietz.pdf

European Commission: Report from the Commission to the Council
and the European Parliament – EU Anti-Corruption Report, Brussels,
03.02.2014; online source: http://ec.europa.eu/dgs/home-

affairs/what-we-do/policies/organized-crime-and-human-trafficking/corruption/anti-corruption-report/index_en.htm
seen 22.10.2014

Engels, Frederick: The Principles of Communism, Moscow, Selected Works 1969, Volume One, p. 81-97, Progress Publishers (original text published in 1847)

Engels to Bloch, Letter of 21/22 September 1890, online source: http://www.marxists.org/archive/harman/1986/xx/base-super.html#n14 seen 23.09.2014

Engels to Carlo Cafiero in Nepal, London, Letter of 28.07.1871. in Marx Engels Werke German edition, Dietz Verlag Berlin, 1975, Vol. 33, p. 664

Engels to W. Borgius, Letter of 25 January 1894. in Marx Engels Werke 1968 (German Edition), Berlin, Vol. 39, p. 206; English online source: http://www.marxists.org/archive/marx/works/1894/letters/94_01_25.htm seen 15.01.2015

Engels to August Beel in Zwickau, London, 18./28.03.1875. Marx Engels Werke, Dietz Verlag Berlin, 1975:, Vol. 34, p. 129

Fu Jing: Urban-rural income gap widest since reform, http://www.chinadaily.com.cn/china/2010-03/02/content_9521611.htm from 02.03.2010, seen 10.10.2014

Liu Jianfei: Democracy and China, New World Press 2011, Beijing

Lukacs, Georg: History and Class Consciousness, Merlin Press, 1967, chapter 1: What is Orthodox Marxism?, p.1 (written in 1919)

Marx, Karl: Critique of Hegel's Philosophy of Right, 1843; chapter 1, The Constitution. Oxford University Press, 1970
online source: www.marxists.org/archive/marx/works/1843/critique-hpr/ch02.htm seen 12.11.2014

Marx, Karl: A Critique of The German Ideology, written: 1845-1846, first published in full: 1932, online source: Marx/Engels Internet Archive (marxists.org), published in 2000

Marx, Engels: Manifesto of the Communist Party. 1848, Chapter 1, online source: http://www.marxists.org/archive/marx/works/1848/communist-manifesto/ch01.htm seen 03.03.2014

Marx, Karl: The Eighteenth Brumaire of Louis Bonaparte. 1852, Chapter 1, online source: http://www.marxists.org/archive/marx/works/1852/18th-brumaire/ch01.htm seen 30.09.2014

Marx, Karl: The Civil War in France; May, 1871, Chapter The Paris Commune, online source: www.marxists.org/archive/marx/works/1871/civil-war-france/ch05.htm, seen 07.2013

Marx, Karl: Capital Volume 1, 1867, Chapter 42: Conversion of Surplus-Value into Capital, Section 3 - Separation of Surplus-Value into Capital and Revenue. The Abstinence Theory. Online source: www.marxists.org/archive/marx/works/1867-c1/ch24.htm seen 01.03.214

Marx, Karl: Capital: An Analysis of Capitalist Production, Moscow; 1959, Volume 1, p. 332

Marx to Paul and Laura Laforrgue in Paris. London, 19.04.1840. in Marx Engels Werke German edition, Vol. 32, p. 673-678

Marx and Engels: "Neue Rheinische Zeitung", Nr. 2, 02.06.1848, online source: http://www.marxists.org/archive/marx/works/download/Marx_Articles_from_the_NRZ.pdf, p.23, seen 20.06.2014

Marx and Engels: Politische Texte Pressefreiheit und Zensur. Iring Fetscher (editor), Europäische Verlagsanstalt Frankfurt, Europa Verlag Wien, Frankfurt, 1969

Marx Engels Werke, Dietz Verlag Berlin, 1970, Vol. 6, German Edition, p. 199-208: "Die Berliner "National-Zeitung" an die Urwähler", Neue Rheinische Zeitung, Nr. 205, 26.01.1849

Marx and Engels: Selected Works, Volume One, p. 81-97, Progress Publishers, 1969 Moscow, article first published: 1914 by Eduard Bernstein in the German Social Democratic Party's newspaper *Vorwärts!*

Mao Zedong: On New Democracy, 1940, online source: www.marxists.org/reference/archive/mao/selected-works/volume-2/mswv2_26.htm, seen 08.2013

O'Brien, Kevin J.: Reform without liberation: China's National People's Congresses and the politics of institutional change. New York: Cambridge University Press, 1990, p. 22

Rigby, S. H.: Marxism and history - A critical introduction, 2nd edition 1998, Manchester University Press, Part One: Marx as a productive force determinist, p. 5-80

Roberts, Dan: Bitter Washington DC mayoral election clouded by corruption claims; The Guardian online, 30.03.2014. online source: http://www.theguardian.com/world/2014/mar/30/washington-dc-mayor-election-corruption-claims seen 22.10.2014

Sedov, Leon: The Red Book On the Moscow Trials, New Park Publications Ltd, London 1980

Wang Fanxi: Trotzki und der chinesische Kommunismus in Trotzki, Leo: Schriften 2, Über China, Band 2.1 (1924-1928), p. 9-50, Rasch und Röhring Verlag, Hamburg, 1990

Wheatley, Alan: In China's economy as elsewhere, the state rises. Reuters Beijing Correspondant, 16.03.2009. online source: http://in.reuters.com/article/2009/03/16/idININdia-38523620090316?sp=true, seen 11.09.2014

Xinhua: China's Communist Party membership exceeds 85 million, Xinhua, Beijing, 01.07.2013.,
http://english.CCP.people.com.cn/206972/206974/8305636.html
seen 25.05.2014

Xinhua: Banking: ICBC announces plan to privatize, delist its HK unit, Xinhua, 11.08.2010
http://www.chinadaily.com.cn/bizchina/2010-08/11/content_11134354.htm seen 25.11.2014

Yang Geng: Defense for Marx. A New Interpretation of Marxist Philosophy, 2003, Canut Publishers

Yao, Kevin; Analysis: China's new privatization plan faces push-back risk, Reuters 24.05.2012
http://www.reuters.com/article/2012/05/24/us-china-economy-investment-idUSBRE84N1N220120524 seen 08.09.2014

Curriculum Vitae

Markus Haunschmid, BA MA

place of birth: Linz, Austria

lives in Vienna

contact: markshauni@gmail.com

Scientific Background

Publication on the subject of Climate Change: "Contradictions in Global Negotiations" at the Second China- EU Social Ecological and Legal Forum, by Renmin University of China Law School and Rosa Luxemburg Foundation, 11.2012

Member of the research staff of the National Defense Academy

Participation at Conferences in China on Labor Relations (Beijing, People's University, 2013), Ecology and Law (Beijing Capital University, 2012; including the publication of the essay "Contradictions in Global Negotiations") and Lenin Today (Wuhan University, 2012)

National conferences as a representative for the Socialist Youth and the Social Democrats in Vienna, International conferences for Society for Society and Politics

Political Background

Organizing member of the China Study Group Europe
(Vienna)
Active member of the
Socialist Youth (Sozialistische Jugend)
Association for Society and Politics (Verein für
Gesellschaft und Politik)
Socialdemocratic Party (Sozialdemokratische Partei, SPÖ)

Former member of the NGO "Civil Service Abroad"
(Auslandszivildienst), Vienna

Student Representative (BA) at the department of Sinology at
the University of Vienna
Pupils Representative at the Lycée Danube in Linz

Educational Background

Master Degree, Sinology in Vienna (MA)
Study of "Marxist Philosophy" at People's University of China
in Beijing
Semester abroad in Shanghai, language classes
Bachelor Degree, Sinology in Vienna (BA) and military service
Lycée Danube, French high school in Linz
Primary school in Linz, Upper Austria

Foreign Languages

German, English, Chinese, French, Italian